THE AUTHOR IN COSSACK COSTUME

ESCAPE FROM
SIBERIAN EXILE

By

JOHN GODFREY JACQUES

in collaboration with
ADELAIDE D. WELLMAN

World rights reserved. This book or any portion thereof may not be copied or reproduced in any form or manner whatever, except as provided by law, without the written permission of the publisher, except by a reviewer who may quote brief passages in a review.

The author assumes full responsibility for the accuracy of all facts and quotations as cited in this book. The opinions expressed in this book are the author's personal views and interpretations, and do not necessarily reflect those of the publisher.

This book is provided with the understanding that the publisher is not engaged in giving spiritual, legal, medical, or other professional advice. If authoritative advice is needed, the reader should seek the counsel of a competent professional.

Facsimile Reproduction

As this book played a formative role in the development of Christian thought and the publisher feels that this book, with its candor and depth, still holds significance for the church today. Therefore the publisher has chosen to reproduce this historical classic from an original copy. Frequent variations in the quality of the print are unavoidable due to the condition of the original. Thus the print may look darker or lighter or appear to be missing detail, more in some places than in others.

Copyright © 2024 TEACH Services, Inc.
ISBN-13: 978-1-4796-1684-8 (Paperback)

Published by

TEACH Services, Inc.
P U B L I S H I N G
www.TEACHServices.com • (800) 367-1844

INTRODUCTION

THE complete story of the sufferings of humanity because of the great world war can never be written. Now and then there comes to us a record of individual experiences which gives something of an idea of the intensity of human passions, and of the hopes and fears and sufferings of the world, during those awful years. Such a story is this.

The hero of this story is a young Russian evangelist of a Protestant "sect." At the outbreak of the war, the priests of the Greek Church, under cover of insuring greater security to the state, took occasion to wreak vengeance on those who had dared to teach the people any other way than that of the established church. Along with many others, our author was banished, being sent to the most northern penal station of western Siberia.

The terrible prisons *en route;* the contact with the worst of criminals; the fellowship with other religious prisoners; the surveillance of tyrannical priests; the sojourn in the lonely forests of the far north with hardened criminals and in proximity to wild tribes; the meeting with a brother minister in the faith who was likewise an exile, with only a few words in passing; the sudden decision to break for liberty; the hasty nocturnal visit home; the six thousand mile flight across Siberia; the perilous and painful journey on foot through Manchuria, over frozen snows, with no guide but the twinkling stars, walking at one time for thirty hours, with torn feet, without rest; the journey to Shanghai; the voyage across the Pacific, with a narrow escape from becoming a prisoner of war,— all this makes the story a most adventurous and thrilling one.

In reading this book, one cannot fail to get a glimpse of the great warfare that is constantly waged between the forces of darkness and light, between superstition and enlightenment, between tyranny and true democracy. The assumption of spiritual control and the coercion of men's consciences by ignorant and even drunken priests, cannot but impress the reader with the utter wickedness of the old *régime* in Russia, and of any system where the state assumes control of religion.

There is also a golden thread of God's care and overruling providence running through this story. The escape, a soldier's assistance offered in a time of greatest perplexity, the "chance" meeting of a boy late at night in a great city, who proved to belong to the same "sect," when there was no other who could shelter the fleeing exile, and many other such things that seemed to "happen" at just the right time, cannot but impress one that God hears the cry of His children in their distress and answers them. "This poor man cried, and the Lord heard him, and saved him out of all his troubles." Psalm 34: 6.

We heartily commend this book to all English-speaking young people, and pray that it may inspire in those who read it such a love for truth, that they too may be willing to suffer, if need be, rather than disobey God.

M. E. KERN,

General Secretary Young People's
Society of Missionary Volunteers.

CONTENTS

I.	WHAT LIBERTY MEANT IN IMPERIAL RUSSIA	17
II.	IN THE CLUTCH OF THE RUSSIAN BEAR	37
III.	BANISHMENT	55
IV.	A PETITION TO THE CZARINA	69
V.	ON THE SIBERIAN BORDER	85
VI.	SEMI-FREEDOM	95
VII.	AN EXILE STATION	105
VIII.	THE "ARRESTED" TESTAMENT	115
IX.	A PENAL ISLAND	133
X.	A FAVOR FROM THE CZAR	145
XI.	LOOKING TOWARD EUROPE	155
XII.	A "WOLF'S PASSPORT"	173
XIII.	THE BEGINNING OF A PERILOUS JOURNEY	183
XIV.	IN DISGUISE	189
XV.	HIDING	205
XVI.	A FUTILE ATTEMPT AT FLIGHT	215
XVII.	AFOOT AND ALONE	221
XVIII.	ENCOUNTERING RUSSIAN GUARDS	243
XIX.	A HAPPY TRANSITION	263
XX.	A PRISONER OF WAR	271
XXI.	LIKE A DREAM	281

ILLUSTRATIONS

The Author in Cossack Costume . . . *Frontispiece*	
Map Showing the Location of Towns Mentioned in the Narrative	16
Odessa	19
In the Crimea	21
A Caucasian Mother	26
A Pass in the Caucasus Mountains	30
The Black Sea Port of Sebastopol	33
The Finest Cathedral in the Caucasus	39
Under Arrest	41
A Russian Family Drinking Their Accustomed Beverage — Tea	45
A Glimpse of Odessa	49
One of the Least Heavily Shackled Exiles . . .	57
A View of the City of Kiev	59
Devil's Bridge, in the Caucasus Mountains . . .	63
General View of the Kremlin, Moscow	67
The Largest Bell in the World, Moscow	68
An Exile in Solitary Confinement	71
A Fine Specimen of Muscovite Architecture . . .	74
"Holy" Moscow	76
Tolstoy	78
Church of St. Basil, Moscow	81
Characteristically Russian	86
The Great Market of Moscow	89
Tomsk University	91
Sleds Used to Transport Exiles	97
A Peasant Abode in Northern Siberia	101
A Siberian Peasant Woman	106
An Ice Jam on a Siberian River	108
Not Handsome, but Happy	111
On the Georgian Road	113
A Russian Family	117
A Typical Peasant Home in Russia	119
A Hollow Log Fishing Canoe on a Siberian River .	123
Weeping, Not Laughing	127
A Russian Village Post Office	131
A Fur Hunter in the Boundless Forests of Siberia .	135
Katun River, a Tributary of the Ob	138
A Siberian Greek Orthodox Priest	142

Nicholas II and His Family	147
Drying Bear Skins	150
Scenery Along the Katun	153
A Siberian Family	157
Tiflis, Capital of Transcaucasia	161
Railway Station at Omsk	165
Hide Market of Kazan Tartars	167
Old-Time Farming Methods	171
On the Volga	176
Mount Ushba	179
A Railroad Bridge Near Ufa	185
Vladivostok	191
Railway Station at Irkutsk	193
Boating on Lake Baikal	195
Railway Station at the Boundary Between Siberia and Manchuria	199
A Mountain Road in the Altai Region	202
Doctor Attending an Exile Who Has Fainted Under the Knout	207
Street Scene in Harbin, Manchuria	210
A Native of the Far Northern Province of Yakutsk, with His Saddle Pony	217
A Makeshift Tent on the Russian Steppes	222
The Troitzko-Sergiev Monastery	227
A Manchurian Convict	233
A Peasant Family	237
Caucasian Tribesmen	241
A Mongolian Plainsman	248
One of the Scenes of Greatest Danger	253
A Village Priest	255
A Small Portion of the Nizhni Novgorod Fair	258
A Chinese City Street	261
Jumping the Rope	268
The Old City of Mukden	269
A Section of China's Great Wall	275
Golden Gate, "the Gateway to Freedom"	279
Nicholas Romanov, the Last of the Czars, in Exile	284
The Ancient City of Tobolsk, the Biblical Tubal	285
On Pacific Union College Farm	287

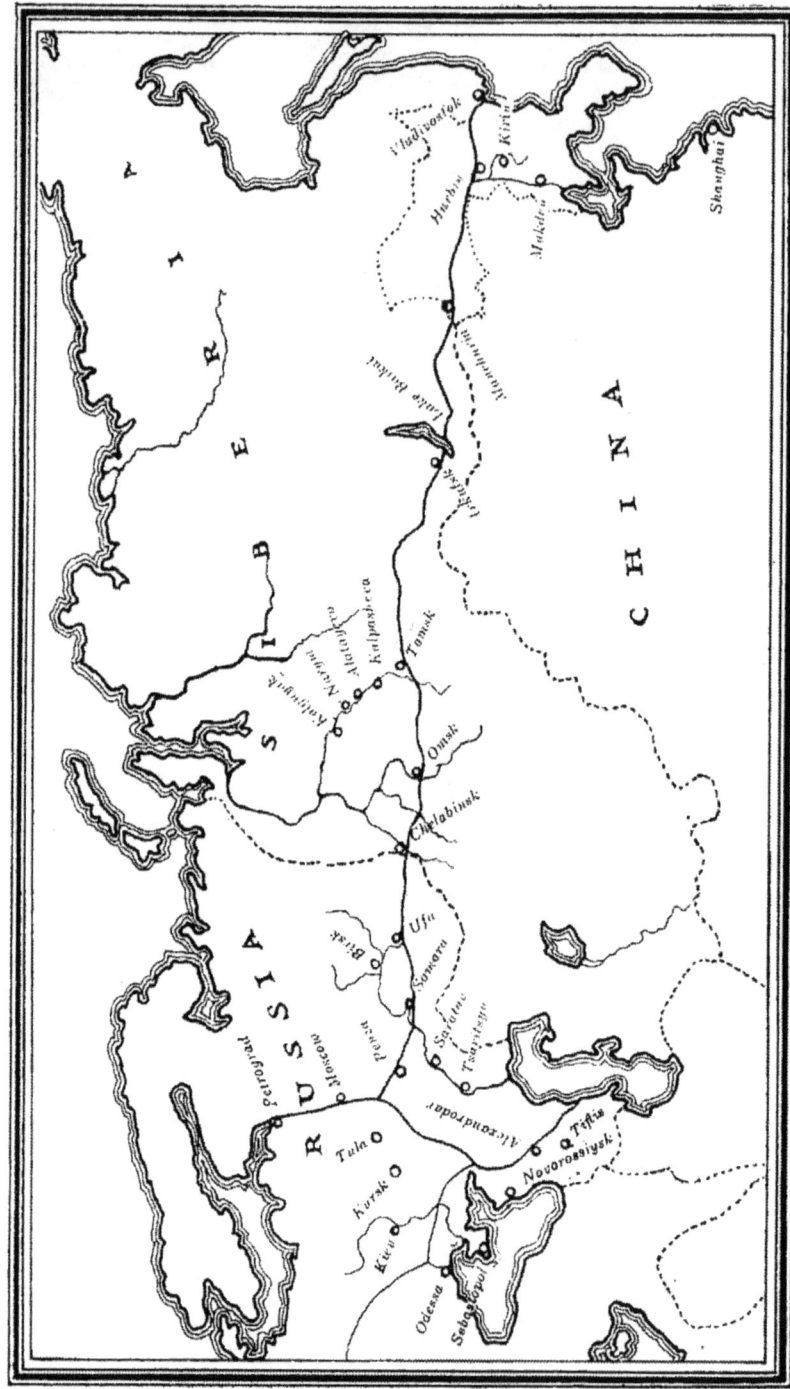

Map Showing the Location of Towns Mentioned in the Narrative

(16)

CHAPTER I

WHAT LIBERTY MEANT IN IMPERIAL RUSSIA

THE giant acacia tree that shaded the doorway of my grandfather's home in the Causasus, shook its yellowing leaves in the autumn breeze like myriads of tiny banners, as I passed out from beneath its sheltering boughs on a September day the year before the beginning of the great war.

In the adjacent chapel — which stood on my grandfather's land — a general meeting had been in progress for some days past. It was attended not only by delegates from different parts of the Caucasus, but also by ministers from other sections of Russia; for this little town of Alexandrodar was to some extent a center for our work in that country, being one of the first places where a church of our faith had been organized in the land of the czars. My parents, when they were young people, became charter members of that church; hence I was reared in the faith we all love.

At this meeting, request had been made that I go and assist our minister located in the Black Sea city of Odessa. The few years that had passed since I finished my school course, I had spent chiefly in evangelistic work in the Caucasus; but consent was given to the proposed transfer, and I was starting for a brief visit to my father's home, a hundred miles distant, before setting out on the longer journey.

When, after spending a day with my parents, I bade them good-by, it was well that we did not foresee the circumstances under which we should next meet.

Instead of taking the ordinary railway route to Odessa, I chose to go by steamer across the Black Sea, as I hoped to be able thus to see my only brother, who was in military service at a post near the shore. I could also, in this way, gratify a long cherished desire to get a glimpse of the beautiful Crimea, the Switzerland of Russia.

Eventually reaching the port from which I should take passage, I sailed away from the shores of my beloved Caucasus. To my deep regret, I was unable to obtain the expected interview with my brother. A matter of less serious disappointment was the fact that the steamer passed some of the most romantic

ODESSA
Stairway leading from one of the principal streets down to the shore of the Black Sea.

(19)

portions of the Crimean coast at night and consequently I did not have a view of them. To compensate myself, as far as possible, for this loss, I was early on deck next morning. The vessel kept close to shore all day, and a delightful panorama moved continuously before us.

With evening and darkness came also rain, in such torrents as to suggest an attempt to raise the sea's level. I found a quiet place in the deck cabin, and there busied myself writing English. From my childhood, the study of that language had possessed an extraordinary charm for me, though I could not have explained why. When only about eight or ten years old, I saved money to buy a large Russian-English dictionary, and that volume I conned most persistently. Doubtless you would hardly have known that it was your mother tongue I was trying to speak; yet those boyish struggles were not without reward when afterwards, under more auspicious conditions, I essayed to master the language that has become to me a symbol of much that is best in life.

But let us resume our Black Sea voyage. Later in the evening, as I was crossing the

IN THE CRIMEA

upper deck in the half darkness, I came into collision with a young man whom I was thus brought to recognize as a former schoolmate of mine. He had been for some years a marine, and that accounts for his preference for the wind-swept deck rather than the cabin.

Not many years before, through the influence of Seventh-day Adventist friends, this young man had been led to accept our faith; and he had since endured great hardships — for to be a Christian in Russia, except in the legal sense, implied persecution in those not remote times.

When, in medieval days, western Europe was emerging from barbarism and adopting Christianity, Russia, not to be outdone, sent commissioners to various countries, to select a new religion for her. The choice fell to Greek Catholicism, and priests were engaged to go from Constantinople to teach the Russian people the forms of that church.

Form and force were predominant features of the religion acquired by the great nation of the north, as was indicated by the practice in vogue in those early days, of driving large companies into the water and compelling them to receive the rite of baptism.

Greek Catholicism was the only Christianity known to Russia until the time of the missionary awakening of the last century, when some of the evangelical churches began activities there.

That the state church had lost none of its dictatorial character in the course of the years, was often demonstrated before the rule of the czars ceased. Near the beginning of the present century, religious liberty for all the "sectarians" was announced; but in reality they had less liberty thereafter than before, when they depended upon secrecy for safety.

The old Russian conception of religious liberty did not include liberty to express one's convictions. Though the imperial government had adopted what was supposed to be a very liberal policy in reference to the "sects," yet, like the Jewish leaders in apostolic times, it required that they should not "speak at all nor teach" of their faith.

The reply in the two cases was the same: "We cannot but speak the things which we have seen and heard." Acts 4: 18, 20.

The first Seventh-day Adventist in Russia, so it is recorded — an aged man who had been to the United States, where he learned our faith — was arrested, after his return to his native land, on the accusation that he was teaching doctrines not in harmony with those of the Greek Catholic Church.

This man stuttered so badly that he could scarcely talk, and to accuse him of conducting any kind of propaganda seemed quite ridiculous.

He had industriously spread our doctrines; but his method was such that he appeared to be the one taught instead of being the teacher. He would ask some one to read to him, indicating what he wanted to hear read — a text of Scripture or other matter bearing on "present truth"; and thus both the reader and any who might be within hearing learned the grounds for our belief.

An effort was made to have the old man exiled; but the judge, for very shame, would not pronounce sentence against him. His affliction served as a safeguard.

When I reached Odessa, among the first persons I met was one of our members who, a short time before, had concluded a two-year term of imprisonment for the Word's sake. His rapid aging during those two years, and the air of constant apprehension that still clung to him, gave a hint of what Russian jail life was. I learned more about it later.

I was soon called to go with one of our ministers to a village some distance from Odessa. There were a number of candidates for baptism; but to administer that ordinance, we must needs go at night to an isolated place outside the town, even choosing a dark and stormy night, in order the more effectually to avoid being observed. Experience had proved that all these precautions were necessary.

In at least one instance, in the Caucasus, a convert who had been baptized into our church, was forcibly rebaptized by priests of the "Orthodox" Church — after the medieval fashion. Others suffered much more severe punishment.

At another town that we visited on this same tour, a child of one of our members had died the day before, and there was much perplexity as to the disposition to be made of the body, the local priest having refused permission for interment in the public cemetery. After our arrival, it was learned that the priest had gone from home. Then the relatives of the dead child quickly and quietly proceeded with the burial. Not infrequently,

A CAUCASIAN MOTHER
She carries not only her babe, but also its cradle.

(26)

bigots of the state church disinterred our dead; and often only by appeal to the civil authorities could we secure a place for burial.

At still another town, a young man and his wife had become interested in the Bible, and had been attending our meetings. The priest, learning of this, came one day to their home to remonstrate with them; and the young man, to justify their course, called attention to numerous scriptures that show our teachings to be sound, and those of the Greek Church the contrary. Thereupon the priest struck the man mercilessly with his walking stick. The terrified wife seized the stick from the hands of the priest, in an effort to defend her husband; but the priest then clutched the heavy crucifix that was suspended from his neck, and with it, beat his victim over the head. The man died a few weeks afterwards, in consequence of this abuse.

After the "sects" began missionary operations in Russia, an organization was formed that was often called "the Black Society." It was made up of zealots of the "Orthodox" Church, whose alleged purpose was the "protection" of that church against "spiritual degeneracy" and loss of members.

This society was specially active in Odessa. Seldom could we hold a meeting without having several of these disturbers of the peace as unbidden guests, and it was their custom to interrupt the services by noisy outcries. They tried also to excite controversy, and thus produce confusion. They often sent women to act as spies on us. These feigned sympathy with us, but listened for any word that might be construed as an offense against the state church.

At a gathering of Baptists near our place of worship in that city, some of these men were asked to leave; and as they did not comply with the request, they were led from the building. One of them then loudly asserted that he had been kicked out by the "sectarians," and he sanctimoniously added that thus had Jesus been treated. In this way, he caused great excitement. The police were attracted to the scene, and much trouble resulted for the Baptists.

These "zealous brethren"—so termed—came to our services in such numbers that their testimony would suffice to condemn any of our speakers they might accuse. Often the leaders of our meetings were arrested at the instigation of these men, the most common charge being that of blasphemy against God and the church; and in case of conviction, the penalty generally was one or two years in jail. There were always some of our people under arrest or in jail in Russia.

But the more vehemently our work was opposed, the more persons seemed impelled to investigate the anathematized doctrines. These persons were surprised to hear, in our meetings, only the pure teachings of the Word; and not a few chose to unite with us. This enraged the priests; and they took revenge, whenever they could, by causing the arrest and imprisonment of our workers.

Still, happily, there were a few men in official position, in both state and church, who stood for justice and equity. When one of our ministers in Odessa was arrested on the charge of "reviling God and the church," the open-eyed old judge, perceiving the groundlessness of the accusation, reprimanded the prosecutors, and acquitted the accused man.

Personally I met a similar spirit of fairness more than once. In a Cossack town where I held meetings not long before going to Odessa, partisans of the state church

A Pass in the Caucasus Mountains
The horsemen are Cossacks—and all Cossacks are horsemen, performing most astounding equestrian feats.

raised a disturbance, and haled me before the magistrate; but when I stated the circumstances to him, he said that I should be allowed to defend my teachings publicly, then the priests should have opportunity to refute what I said, if they could do so.

The people gathered at the church to hear; and the magistrate himself presided, seeing to it that I received just treatment. The priests objected to my going on the speaker's platform, as that place, they said, was holy, and my presence would desecrate it; but there was no other point from which I could be heard well, and the priests were required to grant me equal advantages with themselves.

Not only did the magistrate thus come to my rescue in this crisis, but he also gave me liberty to continue my work in the town; and later a church of our faith was organized there.

In another town in the Caucasus, as I was speaking to a small company of Bible students in a private building, a tall priest entered, and questioned my right to address an audience. In reply, I read Revelation 22: 17, "Let him that heareth say, Come." The priest declared that the text had no bearing on the matter in hand; whereupon the people present — most of them his own parishioners — called to me: "Read it to him again! He doesn't understand." As he still denied the application of the scripture, the people once more called, "Read it again!"

His protests were at last silenced for that time; but at our next meeting, two policemen appeared, and each took hold of one of my arms, as if to lead me away. I reminded them that the law forbade the interruption of a religious service, whether that service were lawful or otherwise; and finally they consented to wait till the meeting had ended. At its close, I voluntarily preceded them to police headquarters.

There, by way of explaining the situation, I gave a *résumé* of the offending discourse. Some priests who were present urged that I be taken away, lest I make converts of the *attachés* of the place. Next I was taken to a police station; and the sergeant, after hearing the case, ordered me to leave the town, else he would send me home by *étape* — that is, with a company of prisoners traveling under guard — which might signify a sojourn of many days in jail on the way.

LIBERTY IN IMPERIAL RUSSIA

I returned to the house where our meetings had been held, and found scores of people waiting for me. They begged that I explain the Scriptures further to them; and regardless of the danger incurred by both speaker and hearers, I did so. We were not molested again; and one of our older ministers later joined me there, and baptized a group of converts.

In a city on the Roumanian border, that I visited after going to Odessa, I was arrested for teaching supposedly heretical doctrines, and the books I had with me were seized. I

THE BLACK SEA PORT OF SEBASTOPOL

was not imprisoned, but had to report at the district headquarters each day for a week. There I learned that my books had been turned over to some of the younger men connected with the office, for examination as to the grievousness of the heresy they contained.

At any time that the higher officers were not present when I called, these young men inquired, with much enthusiasm, concerning the light they had found in the accused volumes; and one of them soon afterwards, as a result of his reading, accepted our faith.

Through his influence, the interest in the truths we hold became so marked as to arouse the priests, and they arranged for a prominent opponent of the sects to go there and combat our teachings. Through the police department, an order was sent for me to meet this defender of nominal orthodoxy; and I could not well refuse to obey.

I had only enough time to reach the place before the hour appointed. As I entered the city, the cathedral bell was sounding its call to the people to assemble for the contest. I did not even know what was demanded of me; but I went direct to a priest of the state church whom I had previously found to be amiable, and from him I learned that three hours each afternoon for three days was to be given to the debate — for a debate the priests had decided there should be — their chosen orator and I to speak alternately for periods of twenty minutes each. Mere boy that I was, it was expected the weakness of my defense would convince the people that I was in error. But the truth of God is not weak; nor did He who has promised to be with those who are called to speak in behalf of the gospel, fail me in those trying days.

The discussion was held in the courthouse, which contained the largest auditorium in the city. This arrangement was made in deference to my expressed wish. I did not want to speak in the cathedral; for there, I knew, the priests would not be willing that I should stand where I could be heard easily.

Written regulations were drawn up, and the opposers of the gospel were obliged to conform to them, the court officials present using their authority on the side of order.

I was the first speaker; and my presentation of the Scriptures did not inspire my antagonist to eloquence. When his turn came to speak, he became greatly confused, and implored the people to pray to the icons for him; and his last period, he spent almost wholly in appeal to these paganish travesties.

The audience manifested strong feeling, some for me, others against me; and probably I should have suffered violence, had not the diocesan, at the close of each session, thrown his long cloak about me and walked by my side. He felt responsible for my safety.

Notwithstanding the consideration shown me at this time, I was forbidden to remain in the city, or to return afterwards to instruct those who might desire instruction. This caused great dissatisfaction on the part of many, specially of the young people, and the priests had difficulty to quell the commotion.

Such was liberty in old Russia.

CHAPTER II

IN THE CLUTCH OF THE RUSSIAN BEAR

ON a December evening in 1914, it fell to me to conduct the service in our chapel in Odessa. The theme of the evening's discourse was the grace of Christ.

There were present in the chapel several enemies of the gospel. Hence I requested our people to disperse immediately at the close of the service, to avoid disturbance; and I likewise went directly to my apartment.

That same night, at half past one o'clock, I was awakened by the ringing of my doorbell. A cousin who was staying with me temporarily, opened the door; and then I heard a clanking of swords, which informed me that my callers were none other than policemen. There were an officer and two subordinates.

I had no doubt as to the object of this untimely visit. As an evangelist of a "sect," I had been brought frequently into contact with the police, and had been arrested a number of times. Yet, though such experiences in the past had always caused a degree of agitation on my part, I felt strangely undisturbed on this occasion. The officer's face seemed to me wholly benign in its expression, and I greeted him with all the cordiality I would feel for an intimate associate.

He accepted the seat proffered him, his assistants standing guard at the door; and in apology for coming at such an hour, he said that he had been at the theater, and the play did not end till one o'clock. I well knew that he had come late in order to be the surer of finding me. My cousin was greatly perturbed at the indications of trouble, but I tried to reassure him.

The officer then exclaimed that it was a pity he must do as he did, but that he was compelled to ask me to arise and dress, preparatory to going with him. When I had complied with his orders, he suggested that I leave my purse and watch, which otherwise would be taken from me when I should be searched at the police station, but that I take a blanket, as a room would be given me there. I knew what sort of room that would be.

Although I comprehended what the events now occurring portended for my future, still

THE FINEST CATHEDRAL IN THE CAUCASUS
The Russian conquest of the Caucasus was marked by the erection of cathedrals, which are therefore termed "military cathedrals."

those initial hours of the long months of suffering I was to endure were a time of peace and restfulness — I would almost say, of joy; and the memory of them was afterwards a source of strength to me.

Before leaving my room, I inquired of the officer the cause of my arrest; but he replied that he did not know, and he in turn asked me what it was. Although I did not know what the specific charge against me was, I did know that the priests of the state church made use of any pretext they could find for bringing accusations against "sectarians." Since the beginning of the war, taking advantage of the increased disposition of the civil and military authorities to restrict individual liberty, they had haled many nonconformist ministers into court on the most groundless charges. Often, too, a mere suspicion was taken as sufficient evidence against an accused person, and he was condemned without a trial.

When my preparations were completed, I sought again to comfort my cousin, then expressed my readiness to go with the officer. The darkness and storm into which I passed from my doorway, were typical of what I was soon to encounter.

My custodian, seeing that I was not disposed to offer resistance, dismissed his men, and called a carriage for himself and me. In

UNDER ARREST
As an arrested person is conducted through Russian streets, with one officer preceding, and another following.

a few minutes, we were at the police station — a place wholly familiar to me before that time.

One lone officer sat sleeping at the desk in the protocol department. I was delivered into his charge by my kindly captor, who then went his way. The desk sergeant, irritated at being disturbed, crabbedly proceeded to write a description of me, and afterwards he summoned policemen from another room to search me. These sleepily performed their task, not neglecting to take from me any article that a prisoner might use in an attempt at suicide, as necktie or suspenders.

Then, at a signal, a guard appeared. Having received his orders, he took me through the building to a rear exit, and thence across a small area to a low structure, where we entered a basement corridor, dark and clammy. Along the corridor were iron doors, on each of which was chalked a number. I afterwards learned that the number indicated how many prisoners occupied the cell.

We stopped at a door that bore a figure 5, and I was given into the care of the guard of that cell. Inside the cell there was a small lamp, which enabled the guard to see the inmates when he peered through a tiny orifice that he opened for the purpose. He turned the lock, lifted the heavy bar, and swung open the door; and there rushed out upon me a stench that thrust me backward as a violent blow would have done.

The guard pushed me inside, and closed the door. For a time, I was overwhelmed by the vile odors that filled the cell. But as I became somewhat accustomed to these, I saw that there were five men crouching on the floor, and one of these I recognized as a Baptist evangelist who had sometimes attended our meetings. Through him, I learned that three of the others also were Baptist evangelists or church officers, while the fourth was an actor who had been arrested as leader in a street brawl. These Baptists had been taken into custody at almost the same hour as I, and they had preceded me to the cell about half an hour only.

The actor was quite hilarious, knowing that his imprisonment was for a few days merely; but the rest of us had no knowledge of what our sentence might be.

To describe that dungeon fully would not be permissible. The room was about six or seven feet wide by ten long. There was a very small barred window close to the ceiling; but it was so obscured by dirt as to afford less light by day than the dingy lamp gave at night. The mildewed walls dripped water. Former occupants of the cell apparently had deliberately planned to make the lot of whoever might be confined there after them, as unbearable as possible. Surely no person could long survive in that pestilential place. For ventilation there was absolutely no provision; and of the filth, I cannot speak.

My courteous cell mates invited me to share their couch of stone. Accordingly, I put my blanket on the floor, which was ice-cold, and sank upon it. As we could not sleep, we whiled away the time talking together. One of the Baptists, pastor of a large German-speaking congregation, could not take part in the conversation, as he did not understand the Russian language, and none of the others, aside from me, spoke German. This man was known among the people of his sect throughout Russia.

The morning seemed weeks delayed; and when it came, we should hardly have been aware of the fact, except that then the feeble light of the lamp was extinguished, and we could hear the sound of the electric cars in the street above.

Our cell door creaked on its hinges, and the guard brought in a pail of hot water, and for each of us a little piece of prison bread. My

A Russian Family Drinking Their Accustomed Beverage — Tea

(45)

hunger was not sufficient to impel me to eat such food, specially in those surroundings.

I hoped that some of my friends might come to me, but none came. The day was almost an eternity to me. At noon, there was brought in a small serving of vegetable soup; and I was then hungry enough to eat. The thought occurred to me that the food provided would sustain life; but not many days afterwards, I discovered that jail fare was much poorer than this "rest house" fare.

In the evening, some food was brought for me alone, having been sent by friends. Through the watchman, I learned that they had tried to get permission to see me, but had not succeeded. However, by persistence, they prevailed in a measure; and the next morning, I was taken to the reception room in the police station, and there was allowed to speak for a few moments with three of the good women of our church, in presence of the assistant chief of police. Women could secure such concessions sometimes when men could not, as it was thought that they would be less likely to connive at the escape of the prisoners. Brief though this visit was, it greatly encouraged me.

The second night, the demand of my system for sleep was so imperative that I could but yield to it, notwithstanding the situation. The next morning, all the prisoners in the "rest house" were taken, under strong guard, into the small inclosure at the rear of the police station; and there, closely watched by policemen, we were privileged to breathe pure air for five or ten minutes. Some of the prisoners from other cells evidently found satisfaction in seeing us in the same position they were in, and they boisterously derided us.

Soon the watch master took his place in the doorway of the cell house corridor, and called to the policemen to drive us in. As the line of prisoners passed him, he told them off one by one, pushing some along, kicking others.

The same morning, our guard informed us that the religious prisoners would be transferred to the city jail that day. This was welcome news. From the time of my arrest, I had received intimations of the verdict that awaited me, and from that verdict I had no hope of escape. But what was inevitable, I preferred should not be postponed. Often I felt to say, Do with me what you will; but what you do, do quickly.

Before being sent to the jail, we were taken to the court room, and there received sentence, although we had had no hearing, nor had we even been told what the accusation against us was. The sentence was, exile to Siberia.

The time was to be as long as war conditions prevailed. This did not mean simply while the war lasted, but until the country should be restored to normal conditions, which we understood might not be till years after the close of the war.

There was little to hope for. I knew that prison bars and bared swords would long be my guardians. Yet in those early days of trial, I realized the constant companionship of Jesus. But there remained to be developed that patience which must characterize the true follower of our Saviour. Often I found comfort in James 1:2-4. I was not permitted to have my Bible, but that text was one I had memorized in previous years.

It was now time for us to start; for a party of exiles was to be taken from the city jail that night, on the way to Siberia, and we were to be of the number.

I was required to leave my blanket at the police station, and consequently I should be

A GLIMPSE OF ODESSA
This is a modern city, as the width of its streets indicates.

without bed or bedding during the long winter journey into the frozen northland.

As we passed through the streets of Odessa, I hoped to catch sight of some of our people, but saw none.

We were led a number of miles outside the city, the jails of Russia, for the most part, not being located within the city limits. Finally we came to a high brick wall, and were halted at the massive gate. The leader of the guard rapped on the gate; and the watchman inside opened it slightly, but on seeing who were outside, closed it again, probably to report to a superior for instructions. The captain of the guard was impatient to be rid of his charge, and he pounded loudly on the gate, while the prisoners, shivering in the cold wind, wished for the shelter of even a felon's cell.

Eventually the gate was opened to admit us; and then we were subjected to that humiliating performance, so often afterwards repeated, the "counting of heads." We were next taken through a succession of gateways in as many high walls surrounding the jail buildings, and at last stopped in the receiving room. There we were searched — the invariable program when a prisoner enters a Russian jail, and also when he leaves. But the treatment here was more humane than that we received in any jail later.

Afterwards our names were entered in a book, and then we were searched again, more carefully, every portion of our clothing being examined. No convict could retain in his possession a particle of metal, not even so much as a needle. Nor was one allowed to keep any money, though each could have held in trust for him at the office of the jail an amount not to exceed about forty cents. Those who were citizens of another country could have ten dollars thus deposited.

As one of the Baptist ministers was a German citizen, the rest of us turned over to him such small sums as we had. With these, during the following weeks, he was able at times to purchase, through the watchman, bread and a few other articles of food, without which it does not seem as if we could have kept alive.

After the searching, we were taken to another building. As we passed along the corridors, we saw behind the iron gratings the most pitiable mortals I had ever beheld — ragged, dirty, emaciated, some of them insane. As they caught sight of us, they crowded up to the gratings, to see what sort of beings their prospective new comrades were.

A door opened, and in a moment we were in the midst of the gaping throng. Besides criminals of various classes, and prisoners of war, there were several young Russian Jews who had returned from France at the beginning of the war, to serve their country, but had been received as foes rather than patriots. Some of their original number had already met what was generally regarded, by victims of the imperial Russian penal system, as a friend — death. Those who still survived sought means of ending their existence.

One aged man in particular among the prisoners excited our pity. He was in utter despair, and must soon have lost his reason. We did our utmost to comfort him; and as he could not eat the abominable prison food, we gave him a remnant we still had of the food that had been brought to us in Odessa. He regained strength and cheer, and was most grateful to us.

About an hour after our arrival at the place, more prisoners came in; and with inexpressible joy, I saw among them my former fellow worker, Elias Gorelic. Delight at seeing this good friend made me oblivious, for the moment, to what his presence there implied to him. He had been arrested at the same hour as I; but his home being in a different section of the city, he had not been taken to the same police station. Other Baptist prisoners raised our number to nine.

At noon, attendants brought into the cell an immense wooden bowl, containing many gallons of thin soup, in which were a few small pieces of potato and cabbage and perhaps a cupful of millet. They brought also smaller bowls and wooden spoons, and undertook to dish out some of the food to each person; but almost before they could begin to do so, there was a mad rush for the bits of vegetables, and even for the few grains of millet. Some of the prisoners threw themselves upon the large bowl, thrusting their filthy hands into it, and there was wild screaming and fighting, in spite of the attendants' free use of cudgel, kicks, and oaths.

When the liquid that remained was divided up, the wretched creatures who had not succeeded in getting any of the vegetables fell to devouring the stuff as a famished wolf devours its prey. One of the lunatics so gorged himself with it that he could not walk. Certainly we did not attempt to eat any of it.

No one could have subsisted on the miserable substitute for food that was furnished us, except for the coarse, half-baked bread served each morning — necessarily only half-baked, else it could not have been eaten, it was so coarse.

There were continual quarrels, and not infrequent blows, among the inmates of the cell. We tried to persuade them to act like human beings, but they appeared almost to have forgotten that they were such.

On the evening after we reached the jail, relatives of some of our company sent food to us, though they were not permitted to see us. Thus we were supplied with a good supper. We shared it with the other prisoners, not only as a matter of humanity, but to prevent their taking the whole by force.

As the night approached, a messenger came to our cell, and called through the bars the names of those who would that night be sent farther on their way into exile. Our party were among those named, and none of us were loath to leave the quarters we then occupied.

CHAPTER III

BANISHMENT

THOSE who were to go were searched again; and before this work was finished, the clanking of chains was heard, and soon the guards were putting shackles upon the exiles. Some were secured hand and foot, while others had only their hands fettered; and the men were then chained in pairs. The prisoner next me having been shackled, I was awaiting my turn, when word came from the captain of the guard, that the religious prisoners should not wear irons.

All were placed four abreast, the high doors swung open, the order was given to march, and once more we were in the open air. It seemed unspeakably exhilarating to me, although the cold wind whipped and penetrated our insufficient clothing. A torch raised before our command, gave to the scene a suggestion of the picturesque.

The preceding day, snow had fallen and afterwards melted, leaving the ground almost impassable. But the soldiers, with unsheathed swords, drove us like cattle through the mud and the darkness.

Beside me walked, panting, an aged prisoner of war. He was too weak to keep up with the others, and one of the soldiers kicked him in the side by way of inducing him to step faster. The poor man sank groaning to the ground; but the column was not allowed to halt, and consequently those behind stumbled over him. After a while, he was again put upon his feet, and driven forward.

We observed several persons following us, and some of the evangelists recognized them as relatives. They were endeavoring to come within speaking distance, but were kept back by the soldiers' swords. The guard hastened our pace to a run. Steam rose from our perspiring bodies. The clang of fetters mingled with the cries of the soldiers.

"Halt!" shouted the captain of the *étape*.*

We were close beside a railway car; and we were herded into it, and thrust into a barred section. In about an hour, the train to which the car was attached moved off.

---

* The French word *étape* has been introduced into the Russian language, as into the English, being used to indicate the quarters where prisoners are lodged when on the way into banishment, also a party of exiles traveling under guard, and further, their transport from place to place.

ONE OF THE LEAST HEAVILY SHACKLED EXILES
Many a Russian has worn a convict's chains simply because he would not let his soul be chained.

Most of the prisoners were smoking, and this made the air of the car suffocating. We traveled thus the remainder of that night, all the next day, and till late in the second evening, when we arrived at Kiev. I was then quite ill.

We were transferred from the railway car to a street car, which had been constructed expressly for prisoners, having no windows, and but one door. I was knocked down in the crowd, and I thought I should be crushed before I could get up.

The old car creaked threateningly, and appeared ready to give way beneath its load. That, I knew, would mean death to some, but I wondered if to others it might mean the possibility of escape.

When the tomb-like car stopped, and we emerged from it, we were outside the city, before a brick wall that inclosed a low, damp building where we were to spend what was left of the night. We had to stand out of doors during the long process of searching.

Having had little food during the day, we hoped for something that night; but we received nothing, as the supper hour was already past.

A View of the City of Kiev

After being put into a cell, our little group had worship together, as had been our wont. The other occupants of the cell were some of the prisoners who had been traveling with us. At no previous time had we thought it wise to invite others to join in our services; but the mood of these men, after the day's wearisome journey, encouraged us to ask if they would like to unite with us, and they all readily assented. We recited, from memory, verses of Scripture, talked a few minutes, and prayed, even the worst of the criminals repeating with us the Lord's Prayer. All this was done very quietly, lest the watchman should interfere.

Before the light of another day had discovered our cell, a guard opened the door, and called for us to make ready to start on the march. After the inevitable searching, we were hurried out of the building, still without food, the breakfast hour having not yet come.

At the gateway, we espied the bent form of an old man; and to each prisoner, as we passed, he gave a tiny loaf of light bread. I inquired the reason for this, and heard the following story about the aged man's benevolence: Years before, his son had been exiled to Siberia; and the father, in remembrance of him, and in sympathy for those who were condemned to a like fate, had stood at that prison gate each morning through all those years, and given a loaf of bread to every exile passing there. He had used up a large share of his property in this way. A delicacy indeed the light bread was to me.

The car that had brought us from the railway station was not large enough to carry our entire number; and going back, I was among those who walked. To be thus in the free air was a privilege, though we were driven four or five miles through the deep snow.

All traffic was compelled to give way to the *étape,* policemen with bared swords clearing a thoroughfare.

At the railway station, we were obliged to stand for an hour in the piercing wind, although those who had walked were wet with perspiration, and all were thinly clad.

The trip from Kiev to Kursk was the least disagreeable part of our journey. Some of our soldier guard were genial boys, and an earnest conversation developed between them and our company of evangelists. They manifested wonderment that persons like us should be banished.

We were assured that we should not have to stay at all in the jail at Kursk, but should keep on to the next stopping place; but on reaching the railway station, we learned that the company with which we were to have gone had already started, therefore we must lodge in the dreaded jail. The hour of our severest trial had struck.

We were taken in charge by soldiers for the forced march of eight or ten miles to the jail. In the searching there, I was the victim of a drunken, inhuman tyrant. He apparently took delight in my suffering. The room being cold, and the asphalt floor wet and dirty, I was so rash as to suggest that I be not required to disrobe, as I had nothing about me that was prohibited. My tormentor was beside himself with rage at such presumption, and raising his fist, declared that he would kill me. But he did not strike. Instead, he demanded that I take off even my underclothing, although that was not customary. Each garment, as I removed it, he threw in a different direction. Then, as soon as he had finished, he began to rave because I was not dressed again.

BANISHMENT

After the searching was ended, we nine requested the jailer to let us have a cell by ourselves. At first, this request seemed to be ignored, and we were put with a crowd of criminals and other prisoners; but after about half an hour, we were taken to a separate cell.

When the old man we had comforted at the Odessa jail observed that we were about to leave him, he clung to us, refusing to be left behind; and he was not hindered from going along. Perhaps the guard did not know that he was not one of our number. This man was

DEVIL'S BRIDGE, IN THE CAUCASUS MOUNTAINS

an atheist, although he showed so emphatic a preference for association with Christians rather than with persons who shared his unbelief.

The cell to which we were assigned was much worse than the one we had left. Water dripped from the ceiling, and the walls were green with mold. The stench was beyond comparison. The only way we could resist the deathly dampness and cold was to run about the room almost constantly. If we stopped for a few minutes, the cold became unendurable. The thought of having to remain there for a week was most alarming. We begged the local inspector to let us have a few pieces of board as a protection from contact with the asphalt floor; but he replied that it was not in his power to do anything for us. We were dumb with agony.

The discipline in this jail was more than ordinarily strict. An officer made a tour of inspection three times a day. The inmates of each cell were warned of his approach, in order that they might stand in line facing the corridor as he passed by. Once when some of those in our cell were too weak and ill to get into position in time, the officer sharply reprimanded us, and threatened to deprive us of hot drinking water. The hot water was our only source of warmth; and furthermore, without it, we could not have eaten the hard prison bread, famished though we were.

Having exhausted our strength in efforts to combat the cold, we sought to devise some method of securing a little rest and sleep. We put some of our coats on the floor, and lay upon them, crowded together literally like sardines, and used the remaining coats as covers. But soon we had to get up and run again.

From the first night, we all had rheumatism as a result of the cold and the dampness. Our throats and ears also were affected. Not till months afterwards was my hearing entirely restored. One week in that damp, loathsome, frigid cell made deep inroads upon our health. In those days, I first learned the real value of prayer. When the wretchedness of my condition overwhelmed me, prayer was the only way of escape from absolute hopelessness.

The promise of transportation from that dungeon after one week, was not fulfilled, and for aught we knew, our confinement there might continue indefinitely.

Meanwhile another detachment of prisoners had arrived. This we learned when one of them was placed in our cell. He had been an imperial Austrian councilor, and freedom had been offered him on condition that he divulge the plans of certain cities in his province. His face told something of what he had suffered for his refusal to betray his country thus.

This man was of impressive appearance, yet wholly unpretentious. He expressed joy at the unexpected companionship he found with us, and thenceforth he was one of us. He took part in our devotional services, evincing perfect confidence in the Scriptures.

Our ninth day here was the acme of our misery. That we could not much longer endure such circumstances was evident. After special prayer together, we determined to appeal to the warden for removal to a less objectionable cell.

That same day, a state inspector visited the jail. As soon as he saw us, he comprehended the seriousness of our situation; and in a few hours, we were taken to another cell.

Up to this time, the local inspector had been very harsh; but after he learned that we were

General View of the Kremlin, Moscow

in prison because of our religion, he was much changed in his attitude toward us.

Our guard in the new quarters was remarkably unlike those we had had before; and each day, he prepared something palatable for us to eat.

We were yet to see why Providence had permitted us to be kept so long at Kursk.

THE LARGEST BELL IN THE WORLD, MOSCOW

CHAPTER IV

A PETITION TO THE CZARINA

NOW we could employ our time to other purpose than that of fighting the cold. Each day, we gave an hour to Bible study together. The German minister was the only one among us who had been allowed to keep a Bible, and the rest of us often wished that in former years we had gained more knowledge of the sacred Word.

One peculiarity of our new cell was most distressing. The ceiling was arched, and the walls were circular. This construction was said to have been intended as a means of torture. A person who has never been subjected to the ordeal, cannot imagine the effect produced upon the nerves as the eyes follow the circling lines, with no place to rest. In some instances, this has even caused insanity, or at least contributed to it. Any one who has lain ill in a room where the wall paper was of intricate pattern, and has spent weary hours trying to trace out the design, will not think that statement an exaggerated one.

At about this time, we asked the privilege of sending a petition to the governor-general of the Odessa war zone. The object of the petition was, to get leave to make the remainder of our railway journey as ordinary passengers, under guard, as exiles sometimes did, we to pay the traveling expenses.

This request brought us to the attention of the warden, and frequently thereafter he sent for some of us to come and talk with him on religious subjects. On the wall of his office hung a portrait of the former chief inspector of the jail system of all Russia. This high official was in sympathy with the sectarians, and attended their services in Petrograd. When the warden was informed of this, his interest in us appeared to increase.

Some of the other officers of the jail also gave evidence of being well disposed toward us, and came to our cell repeatedly to talk with us. Opportunity was given us to write postal cards or short letters to our friends; but of course these brief missives were censored, and if anything had been found in them that the prison authorities did not approve, we should have paid a heavy penalty.

Soon after Christmas, the priest of the parish in which the jail was located, made his yearly rounds to "bless" the cells. We were

An Exile in Solitary Confinement

notified beforehand of his coming, and all stood during his presence, except one man who was not well. Others of us had urged this man to let us help him to stand while the priest performed his ceremonies; but as we had been treated leniently for some time, he was emboldened to disregard the requirements.

The policeman in attendance on the priest was enraged at such a breach of discipline, and we feared he would have the transgressor put into a dark dungeon. These dungeons were so low a man could not stand upright in them; and to the darkness, the noxious odors, the suffocating lack of air, cold, hunger, solitude, and the dampness caused by frequent flooding of the floor, was added the prospect of never again knowing any other existence.

The ceaseless rattling of the fetters on our fellow prisoners made a sound pitiful to hear. Such a sound heard in a machine shop or a foundry would not be particularly painful; but when we knew that it signified a cruel burden borne perhaps for many years, reducing wrists and ankles to skeleton-like size, it was truly pathetic.

On stated days, we were taken into the courtyard of the jail for a few minutes' breathing spell. At these times, we delighted in seeing the crows that came for the crumbs we had saved for them. They brought to us, in return, a suggestion of joyous freedom.

Thus three weeks wore away after our change of cell. As each week passed, we were told that on the next, we should leave this place. Transportation from jail to jail was not an agreeable experience. Often it involved kicks and beatings, and divers forms of discomfort. Yet we longed for it more impatiently than a child longs for an expected holiday.

On the last day of our sojourn at Kursk, the son-in-law of the German pastor, and the daughter of another of our number, came to the jail, and an interview with their relatives was granted them. They brought food for us all, sufficient for a few days; and blankets and extra clothing, such as we had not been permitted to bring with us. Thus we saw one reason why God had let us be detained so long there; for the extreme cold of the Siberian winter would have mocked at the light garments we had worn.

These visitors also brought money to pay our fare for the rest of our railway journey,

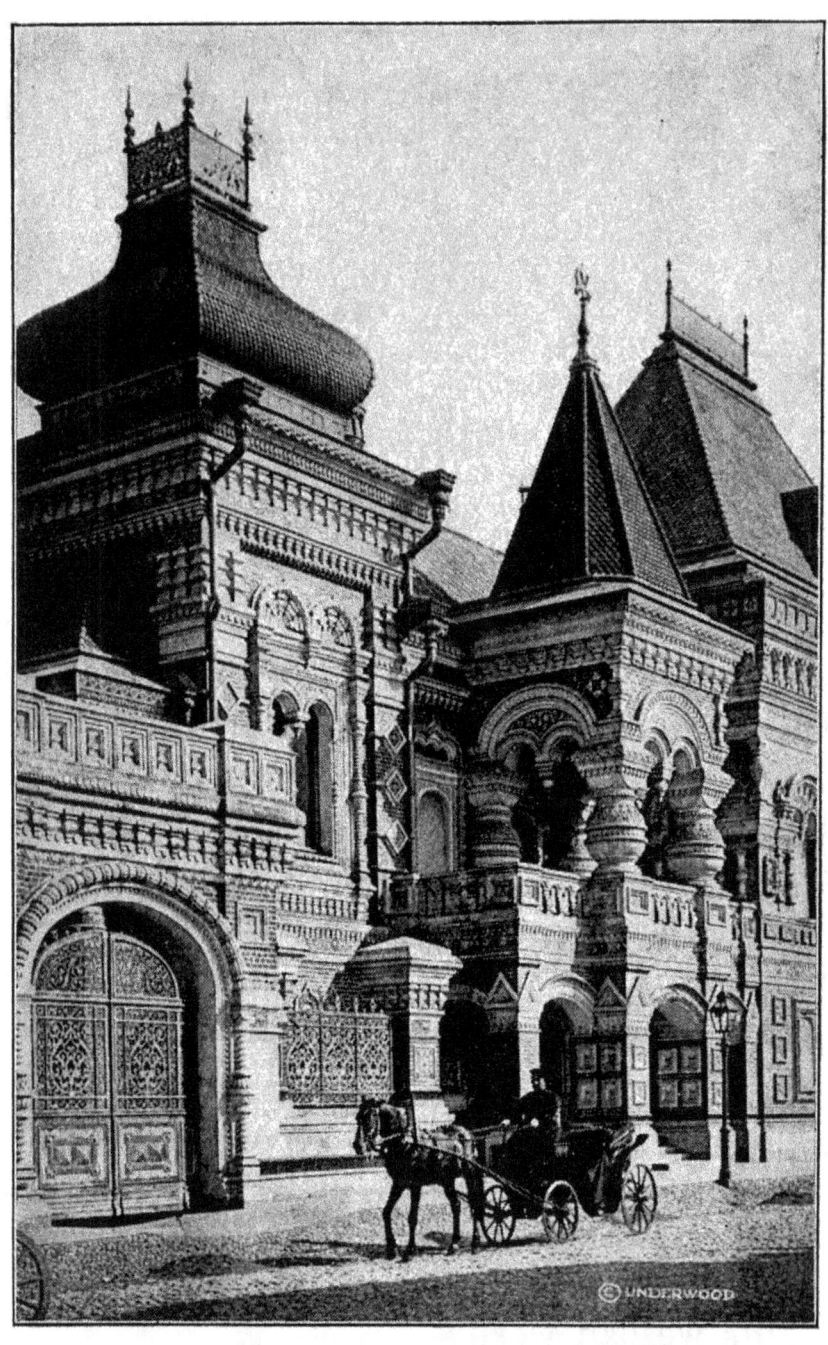
A Fine Specimen of Muscovite Architecture, the Residence of a Moscow Merchant

in case the governor-general should consent to our traveling by passenger train; but apparently we were not in the category of prisoners to receive any favors from him.

This visit had still another and far greater significance. After the first interview, we prepared a petition to the czarina, in which we respectfully asked that our sentence be modified so that we should be sent to some station in European Russia instead of the far northern part of Siberia. Then the father of the young woman obtained permission to shake hands with her at the farewell interview; and as he clasped her hand, he left in it the petition, which had been written on thin paper, and tightly folded.

She afterwards transmitted a copy of this to a lady of the imperial court, who was herself a sectarian; and through this channel, it reached the czarina, and ultimately the czar. This meant much to us later.

The night after our visitors left, we were awakened at about two o'clock, by a call to march. Overjoyed, we sprang to our feet; and quickly our packs were on our backs and we were awaiting the opening of the doors. During the searching and the forming of

"Holy" Moscow

the command, I observed crouching on the floor some women prisoners,—distressed looking creatures, one of them, who had a babe in her arms, being evidently near death. It would not seem as if any heart could be unmoved by the sight. Yet no mercy was shown to these women.

After we had been taken into the prison yard, the warden came out, and called to us religious prisoners by name; and when he had found us, he presented to us three copies of the New Testament.

An hour's tramp through the snow brought us to the railway station. Our leader displayed more consideration than we had received on like occasions before; for he found shelter for us in the station, in order that our perspiring bodies should not be exposed to the intense cold outside.

There was questioning among the prisoners as to whether we were to be taken through Moscow; but when we were not far from that city, our course was changed, so that we passed to the east of that historic capital of Great Russia.

We arrived at Tula late in the evening, and were marched five miles to the jail.

TOLSTOY, WHOSE ESTATE WAS NEAR TULA

There we were put in a large cell with about one hundred criminals. Among these were many thieves, who gathered in groups, each of which had its leader. Some of them were laying plans for their next campaign — for their depredations did not cease in prison. They were on very amicable terms with the jailers; and we learned afterwards that they divided their booty with them in return for certain concessions.

While the prisoners lacked food, they did not lack

tobacco; and the tobacco fumes increased the foulness of the air. Many of the prisoners were tuberculous, and other communicable diseases were rife.

After three days, we were taken from this place, and headed toward Samara. The soldiers in charge of the *étape* were merciless.

We had been told that there would be a change of guard at Penza, but that no transport ever stopped at the jail there. However, when we had waited an hour at the railway station, for the guard that were to take us to Samara, and still they did not come, we were driven to the Penza jail.

As we stood before the gate, a little girl appeared with a package of bread, which she wished to give us; but the soldiers roughly ordered her away. She left sorrowfully, disappointed that she could not fulfill her mission of mercy. Possibly she had heard of the benevolent old man at Kiev, and had thought to emulate his example.

At the jail, we waited another hour or two. We were informed that the soldiers were taking their baths, hence the delay. When at last they were ready, we gladly continued on our way.

We crossed the Volga, and arrived at Samara in the evening, in a heavy snowstorm. From the railway station, the lights of the prison were pointed out to us. But to us, they were not cheerful lights.

We waded through snow knee-deep to the prison, and after the usual delay, were admitted through the first gate, then a second, and still a third, and afterwards into the searching hall.

The food in this jail was clean in comparison with that in the other jails, the bread was more edible, and cooked grains were provided. If all the food had been served to the prisoners individually, no one would have lacked seriously. But only the bread was thus portioned out. The other food was brought into the cells in bulk, and the most lawless prisoners got nearly all of it.

The cells were the most habitable we had yet occupied. But all classes of prisoners were crowded together; and during the last days of the sixteen that we spent there, there was no room even to move about, and hardly enough to sit down.

The thieves carried on their work here as at Tula. One of them feigned interest in the gospel; but when he found that his pretense did not make me relax my vigilance in guarding my belongings, he was in a rage, and vowed he would take revenge on me when we reached our destination.

CHURCH OF ST. BASIL, MOSCOW

Thieving is as verily a habit as is the use of stimulants. Some of these confirmed thieves were really unable to be quiet after night came on. Though they might want to sleep, they seemed impelled to creep about and seek pillage.

The Baptists who were with us wrote post cards to friends in Samara, and these friends came to see them at the jail. Gorelic and I inquired whether there were any Seventh-day Adventists in the city; and learning that there were, we sent a request that some of them visit us. A few days afterwards, our minister who was stationed in the place, called upon us. His wife had implored him not to do so, fearing that he too might be arrested if he thus identified himself with us; but his conviction that he ought to come was so strong he could not refuse to heed it.

Gorelic being too ill to go to the visitors' room, I went alone to meet our guest. The interview could last only a few minutes; and even during that little time, we were separated by two sets of grating, with guards between. Not many words were spoken. Yet the comfort it gave me simply to look into the face of this brother, was beyond expression. When I was taken back to my cell, I endeavored to communicate to Gorelic the encouragement I had received.

Our good brother had brought us food and also some money. As we were not allowed to take the money, we asked that it be kept for us at the office of the jail, and were told that it would be; but we never saw any of it again.

Most of the food was stolen from us in our cell. If we had given some of it to the thieves at the outset, we might have fared better.

In one large cell of the Samara jail was a Prussian pastor with his whole flock, who had been taken as prisoners of war — men, women, and children, some sick, all dirty, ragged, and half starved. The aged cleric found diversion in keeping count of the vermin he caught in his clothing. The number was in the thousands when he showed us his record.

The hunt for body vermin — though not the tally — was necessary in self-defense; for so numerous were these parasites, that if not destroyed, they would sap one's very life.

One day, we were startled by shrieks from one of the other cells. Jailers ran in the direction from which the noise came; and soon we saw them hauling a prisoner down the stairs. The poor wretch's mind had given way under the conditions to which he had been subjected.

When Gorelic had partially regained his strength, I became ill. Fortunately, as both were not helpless at the same time, we could wait upon each other in turn.

Some of the prisoners who arrived later than we, were removed sooner. This, to be sure, tended to discourage us. The covetous chief jailer knew that we had a small sum of money on deposit at the office, and he warned us that unless we gave him an amount which he specified, he would see that we remained long where we were. When, after a little more than two weeks, we were called to transport, he tried frantically to get hold of some of our little store, but did not succeed.

CHAPTER V

ON THE SIBERIAN BORDER

THE train soon bore us over the Ural Mountains, the natural frontier between Europe and Asia. We received the acceptable tidings that at Chelabinsk, we should not be taken into the jail, but should stop at the prisoners' transportation station until the next *étape,* a few hours later.

We were marched through the city, a distance of about five miles. Only with difficulty could I walk, being half sick; and my pack seemed an almost unbearable weight.

As it was Sunday, many people were riding on the streets; and there were exclamations of delight and clapping of hands, for we were thought to be war prisoners, and our presence was regarded as evidence of the success of the Russian troops. In truth, some of us were loyal Russian citizens.

At the transportation station, we were delivered over to the care of humane soldiers. We had heard before that the Siberians were more merciful toward exiles than were the Russians, and this assertion was verified in our contact with them. An explanation of their considerate disposition may be found in the fact that many of them had themselves been exiles, or were descendants of such.

Announcement was made that there were too may prisoners for one transport, and some must go to the jail and wait another week. Our company were among those to wait. With the memory of our recent experiences still very vivid, the thought of having to undergo a repetition of such experiences was most depressing.

The scanty baggage we carried — bound upon our shoulders with thongs — was mi-

CHARACTERISTICALLY RUSSIAN

nutely searched. Then we were put into a cell with the same class of criminals that we had encountered at Samara. In this cell, there were "bunks"— so decorous a term as "berths" would be a misnomer. We could not get possession of any of these; but this was not wholly a misfortune, for we secured a place near the bars, where the watchmen could see us plainly, and thus we had their protection. The watchmen in this jail were apparently honest; yet, as they could not see clearly so far into the poorly lighted cell as the "bunks" were, the thieves operated there diligently.

One morning, when the inspector made his regular circuit, an Austrian prisoner of war reported to him that one of the other prisoners had stolen some money that the Austrian had concealed in his clothing. In acknowledging that he had secreted anything about his person, the man became liable to a penalty of at least two weeks in a dark cell. And further, the thief and his colleagues threatened him with dire punishment for accusing them. To avert these consequences, he retracted his statement. But even after that, the thieves beat him most brutally.

Another morning, one of the ministers discovered that the soles of his shoes had been cut away in the night. The motive doubtless was, to find any money that might have been hidden inside.

During the first part of our stay here, the warden would not permit the watchman to buy food for us with the money held in trust for us in the office of the jail; but later, permission was given for him to do so. The price charged us was probably three or four times what the watchman paid; but in reply to a demur on our part, he tauntingly suggested that thereafter we go and make our own purchases.

When the time set for us to leave Chelabinsk had passed, and still there was no indication that we should go soon, a riot was started in our cell. The prisoners insisted that they be allowed to see the warden. He came, together with his subordinate officers, all armed, and they entered the cell. The spokesman of the prisoners then stated their demands. The warden was very conciliatory while standing among that hundred reckless men, and he promised to do all he could to hasten the time of their going.

THE GREAT MARKET OF MOSCOW

Nowhere else had our stay among the criminals been so trying. They were very bold, stealing even in the daytime. I kept close to my baggage all the while; but this provoked their ire, and they became intent on doing me injury. The misery of our surroundings would have been unendurable but for the comfort bestowed by Him who is rightly called "the Comforter."

I met in this cell a prisoner of war — a Prussian peasant — who, with his wife and children, had been transported back and forth from jail to jail, seemingly for no purpose but to wear their lives away. There were many others equally unfortunate. One man was dying before our eyes. The feet of another were frozen, and he could not stand. He was sent to the jail hospital, which was another step toward death.

While we were with these men, they joined us each day in worship, and some evinced a real respect for Christianity. One aged man was inconsolable when he was taken from us. He said he wished to remain with us till he should die, or his condition should be bettered.

After spending two weeks at Chelabinsk, we left for Tomsk. This journey required three days. The soldiers had told us that it was likely we should stop at the two jails at intermediate stations; but we passed them by, and not at all reluctantly. Our spirits rose hourly, for we hoped to quit cell life soon — though not free, yet no longer to be confined behind prison bars.

We reached Tomsk at night. When the cold air struck our lungs, we could hardly breathe. The temperature was forty degrees below zero.

We were formed into orderly command, four abreast, and were thus taken to the jail. As the dry snow creaked noisily under our feet, the sound was echoed by the forest. The bright moonlight shone on the snow-laden fir trees; and notwithstanding the wretched ap-

TOMSK UNIVERSITY

pearance of the prisoners, the scene on the whole impressed me as really pleasing.

One man, being lightly clad, succumbed to the cold, and fell by the way. He was dragged to a sled in the rear, which was intended for such emergencies.

The jail was a large, white building; but its color did not typify what we found within. Our small company had hoped that like the political prisoners, we might have a separate cell; but instead, we were put with a gang of criminals. These seemed to consider the cell as their own, and us as intruders. They dealt out the food, giving us only very small servings; but we accepted this arrangement without protestation, knowing that any complaint would make matters worse. The one distinguishing feature of this jail was that the food — what little we had — was fairly edible.

One of the greatest boons of our prison existence was the few minutes spent in the small, high-walled yard two or three times a week. Though we were kept walking in a circle, under guard, yet no wealth could have purchased from us this respite.

On our third day at Tomsk, we were transferred to a cell in which there were only prisoners of war. This was a decided relief to us, as we had been compelled for months to mingle with the worst of criminals. After that, we did not see them except when taken into the area.

In one cell that we passed at such times was a most harrowing spectacle — a company of war prisoners who were dying of filth and hunger.

We had been only about a week in the jail at Tomsk, when the jailer opened our cell door, and read the names of those who would the next day be transported; and our names were on the list. There is nothing to which I can compare our joy at the prospect of leaving this, the last jail on our route. We knew that the cold would be pitiless five hundred miles farther north, where we were to be stationed, and that the transport by small sleds would involve much suffering; but that did not lessen our enthusiasm at the thought of getting into the free outdoors.

One thing for which our little group had prayed was that we should not be separated. That we had kept together so long was extraordinary; for in many instances, families were broken up.

On our last evening in jail, when we had worship, several of the other prisoners wept because we should have no more such occasions together.

As we left the jail, we noticed a significant change — the soldiers' swords were no longer bare, but were in their sheaths; and for the transport of about twenty-five prisoners, there were only two guards. Precautions against the escape of prisoners were little needed in that snow-bound region.

CHAPTER VI

SEMI-FREEDOM

HAVING for so long a time scarce been permitted to make a move without orders, we could not readily accustom ourselves to any degree of freedom. And freedom this was to us, in contrast with cell life. Our march through the city seemed almost like a triumphal procession.

We were taken to the prisoners' transportation station to await *étape*. The windows and doors of this building were barred, yet it was different from the prisons.

On the wall, we found written, in pencil, "You will receive nineteen rubles for warm clothing, and about eight rubles a month for food." To this was signed the name of a prisoner who had occupied the same cell as we at the last jail, but had started forward the previous day. Before he went, we had requested that he leave some message for us, at the first opportunity, as to how he fared; and this was the way in which he had complied with our request.

One by one, we were conducted to the office of the *pristav* of Narym, in an adjoining building. There our places of exile were announced; and to each of those who most lacked clothing, nineteen rubles was given for the purchase of additional garments. One elderly clerk declared that no money should be given me, and he talked excitedly of the great war expenses of the government. But he left the room before I did; and after he had gone, a younger clerk gave me the regular quota.

Later the guard took us to the market, where we bought felt boots, fur mittens and caps, and such other necessary articles as our means would allow. Some of us afterwards asked permission to go to the post office; and this being granted, we hired a sleigh, and with a guard, flew off through the streets. Literally like flying it seemed to me, so delightful were the comparative liberty and the fresh air.

It was dark when we returned to the station, and horses and sleighs were in readiness for us. As we were taking our places in the sleighs, one of the Baptist evangelists came to us, in deep distress, to say good-by. A telegram had been received at the station, demanding his return to Odessa, for trial on a charge similar to that which had sent him into exile. Back over the dread route by which we had come, he was taken. After all this, he was acquitted of the charge; but he was nevertheless obliged to make the terrible journey to Siberia again, because of the original sentence.

Our long line of sleds moved off. As I was not well, the leader of our guard thought to

SLEDS USED TO TRANSPORT EXILES

show me exceptional consideration by giving me a place in a comfortable sleigh, with an aristocratic prisoner. But this man was an atheist; and his talk was so offensive to me, that I preferred less pretentious company. So I left him, and rode with Gorelic, in a small sled.

Under a starlit sky, we rode out upon the limitless fields of snow. When occasionally our driver stopped, we knew that a sled ahead of us had upset. Such occurrences were frequent, as the sleds were very narrow.

One of the prisoners of war seemed to be perishing from cold. Such of my clothing as I dared spare, I gave to him, or surely he would have frozen to death.

Sometimes we thought we saw wolves, and possibly we did; but in some cases, the dark objects we had supposed to be wolves, proved to be only bushes.

It was eleven o'clock when we reached the village where we were to spend what was left of the night. The people in the house where we stayed, regarded us quite indifferently; for a company of exiles stopped there every night. After warming our chilled bodies, we found places on the floor to sleep.

Early next morning, we were called to transport. At each village at which we halted—ten to twenty miles apart—there was a new relay of horses, also a change of drivers.

Some of the way, the snow lay smooth and level; but elsewhere it was heavily drifted, forming high ridges and deep valleys.

After the first night, we traveled mainly on the ice of the Ob. This river is the only highway in that part of the country, summer or winter. The population is very sparse, there being only little settlements along the banks. Scattered timber began to be seen, and a thicker growth as we advanced.

These were the last days of February. The ice was then about ten feet thick. Had we not been detained at Kursk, we should have reached this stage of our journey at a time when the temperature was far lower, and our supply of clothing less adequate. We had chafed and almost despaired at the long confinement in prison; but now we realized that it was well the Father had seen fit not to keep us from the trial, but rather to sustain us through it.

On the second and third days of our journey by sleds, I was quite ill. The third night, we were at Kalpasheva; and as I then had a high fever, it seemed necessary that I accept the counsel of our captain, and remain at the little hospital there. But Gorelic would not consent to our separation. He did what he could for me during the night; and the next morning, he laid me in our narrow sled, and with the aid of a prisoner of war whose good will we had won, he endeavored to keep me from falling off the unstable conveyance. He had obtained a sled that had a frame of reeds, and this made it more secure. Still, again and again I rolled off into the snow. This, however, was not a grave catastrophe.

Where we spent the next night, there were no beds, and the only food was fish, which I could not eat. How I craved some broth or other light food! But where was it to be found? Gorelic had a difficult task in caring for me.

On the morning of the fifth day, I was somewhat better. That night was the last of our journey. The room in which we stayed was well heated; but we were obliged to open the doors and the windows, and let the frigid air in, as a means of driving the thousands of bedbugs to their retreats in the log walls.

When morning came, my condition was further improved. Our hostess supplied us with milk and cream; and for the first time in four days, I was able to eat.

The people thereabouts were all Ostyaks. This tribe, not many years ago, were converted to Christianity — nominally, and in part forcibly. In some of their homes are still reminders of their former paganism, including images, which are said to be worshiped in secret.

The young horse attached to our sled was not inclined to keep to the beaten track, choosing instead to flounder in the deep snow.

A Peasant Abode in Northern Siberia

Consequently the others went on without us. Only with Gorelic's aid did the driver finally get control of the animal.

At noon, we left the river, with its bordering forest, for the open snow fields. Erelong from out the whiteness appeared a small village, and we were told that it was our destination — Alatayevo. As we came nearer, we were surprised to find such fair looking houses. They were built of logs; but as timber cost nothing except the labor of getting it out, the buildings were of generous size.

One more snow valley, little horse, and we shall be there! Away he gallops, to overtake the others. Some of the sleds ahead of us were overturned, throwing the occupants into the snow. Others of the exiles laughed at the trifling mishap. They had not laughed in months before.

We stopped in front of a house which I learned was that of the town constable. There, for the last time, we were counted, and then our guard dismissed us to find rooms for ourselves.

We now had to part with our fellow prisoner the imperial councilor. This we did with sorrow. He was taken farther north.

With Gorelic and the young man who had helped him to take care of me, I started in search of a room; but after going a few rods, I was too exhausted to walk farther, and said that I would wait for them at the house where we then were. The two others continued the search, but later they returned and engaged a room where I had stopped. We were to pay a monthly rental of seventy-five cents each. Afterwards we were convinced that our location was providential.

Our host was celebrating his birthday anniversary, and guests were present at tea. We were invited to eat with them. In these isolated sections, every holiday is accounted holy. Such superstitions are fostered by the priests, as a means of gaining a stronger hold upon the people.

I was inexpressibly relieved that I need no longer see prison bars and bared swords, or hear the clank of fetters and the harsh cries of the watchmen. Henceforth our watchmen saw us but once a day.

Had we been delayed a few days more, I should have been too ill to travel. The second day after our arrival, I could not rise. My fellow exiles did everything they could for my comfort. They gave me the one bed in our room, while they slept on the floor. They also purchased material of which they made a "tick," or mattress cover; and this they filled with wild hay, which was abundant there. A luxurious bed I thought it, after having so long slept on the asphalt floor of a prison cell.

CHAPTER VII

AN EXILE STATION

THROUGHOUT March, I was so ill that I had to lie in bed nearly all the time — a result, no doubt, of the exposure and want of the preceding months. For a still longer time, I could hear continually, with all the vividness of actuality, the rattling of shackles and the shouts of guards which had sounded in my ears during those months.

Late in April, I was well enough to walk a short distance, with help, along the trail that led through the deep snow between our lodgings and the river. The sunshine was then bright and cheery, though the cold was still severe.

Even while suffering physically, I was happy; for though under guard, yet I could breathe the pure out-of-door air, and go about freely within narrow limits.

In Siberia, as in many parts of Russia, the people are unaccustomed to sleeping in beds. A bed is commonly included in a bride's dower, but it is merely for display. When we were strong enough, we bestirred ourselves to get something else to sleep on than the one poor semblance of a bed which our room contained. The people were astonished that we should think of indulging in such luxury; but we deemed it a necessity, for protection from the cold that came through the crevices in the rough floor.

Although there was a boundless supply of timber in the dense forests all about, the deep snow prevented our securing any of it; but we found birch saplings, and bent these in such a manner as to give a springiness to the

A SIBERIAN PEASANT WOMAN
Doing the weekly washing in the river when the temperature is thirty-five degrees below zero.

beds we manufactured of them. At first, our attempts aroused much ridicule; but after a while, other of the exiles tried to imitate our products.

A perplexing problem was, how to defend ourselves against the hordes of bedbugs that assailed us at night. To rid our room of these pests was impossible, as the log walls furnished innumerable hiding places for them. By experiment, we learned that the creatures could not swim. So we set the legs of our bedsteads in cans of water, and thus were insured against attack.

The people about us marveled when they learned of this device. All their lives, they had been tormented by these pestiferous insects, often being ill in consequence. Yet they had never resorted to even so simple a plan of defense.

Immediately after arriving at our destination, we had written home; but not till near the first of June did an answer reach us. In the spring months, the breaking up of the ice makes the river impassable for either sleds or boats; and these northern stations are entirely cut off from the world during that period.

For about three months of the summer, river steamers come up from the south, bringing flour and other supplies, and taking in exchange pine nuts that the settlers gather from the forests. Some years there are none of these nuts to be found; but one good crop pays for provisions for a number of years.

The large rivers of Siberia all flow toward the north. In spring, the ice near the sources of the rivers breaks up fully a month earlier than that at their mouths; and the broken ice, as it is carried northward by the current, is forced beneath the still solid ice of those colder latitudes, causing it to burst with a tremendous boom, like that of heavy thunder.

An Ice Jam on a Siberian River

This broken ice forms immense dams, which cause the rivers to overflow thousands of square miles of the tundra. For this reason, only the small patches of higher land along the rivers are inhabited, except by the native Tungus. The people of that wild tribe travel over the swamps in summer, as over the snow in winter, on skis.

The settlements become little islands when the tundra is flooded; and there is never any certainty as to the height at which the water will cease to rise. The people always have their canoes ready for use in case the water should reach the houses.

In the month of June, the mouths of the rivers become free of ice. Then the water from the tundra flows back to the river beds. The retreating water leaves a thick mud over the land. In the remaining six or eight weeks of the summer, there grows up in this mud a coarse grass, man-high, which is the only fodder obtainable for horses and cattle.

The leanness of the stock, however, is caused not so much by lack of food, as by the cold. Each year, many domestic animals freeze to death. Still others fall victims to the big Siberian bears.

As the horses and the cattle must be kept in stables throughout the long winter, they suffer from the confinement; and the owners let them out in the spring as soon as patches of ground can be found where the snow is sufficiently melted off.

Not long after we reached Alatayevo, a cow that had been let out for exercise, was found dead, the body partially devoured. The men of the village organized a bear hunt; and eventually they found the guilty beast — a big female bear.

With four or five cubs, she was snugly sheltered in a natural tent formed by the drooping branches of a pine tree. The weight of the snow on the branches bent them down so that their outer ends reached the ground, but no snow could sift through the thick foliage.

The old bear was killed, and the cubs were captured. One of the cubs was given to the children of the family that the chief of our guard lived with, and it became very much of a pet. I used often to see it when I went to call on the guard.

I know of no more charming pets than young bears. They are very playful — more

AN EXILE STATION

so than any kitten — amusing themselves for hours at a time by turning somersaults, or clutching the head in the hind paws and rolling over and over like a ball, or performing other comical "stunts." They are also very chummy with their human friends.

This one soon learned to take milk from a bottle. Having been accustomed, bear-like, to sucking its paws, it had little difficulty in substituting the bottle rubber for them.

Still more, it soon acquired the art of holding the bottle in its paws. A ludicrous figure the little fellow made, sitting up on his

Not Handsome, but Happy

haunches, with the bottle in his big paws. And even little bears have very big paws.

When we had been in Siberia about two months, all the exiles in our village were summoned to the house of the head man of the station, to get our apportionment of money for the time we had been in exile — seven rubles and twenty copecks a month for each person. Later fifty copecks extra was added. Ordinarily one ruble is equal to half a dollar of American money; but because of the war, the value had then fallen to about a third of a dollar. No allowance was given in advance.

Meanwhile Gorelic and I had received a few dollars from home. Exiles were permitted to have only small amounts, any larger sums that were sent to them being confiscated. We purchased a few dishes, also fish and meat, and sometimes a little milk.

The fish and the meat, and even the milk, were frozen. Farther south, where there are markets, milk is sold in solid blocks, carried by a string or a stick, one end of which has been frozen into the block.

The people of Siberia subsist almost wholly on meat, fish, and tea, with an imitation of bread. This last is made largely of small wild

ON THE GEORGIAN ROAD

This road, about two hundred miles in length, is the principal highway across the mountains from the Caucasus to Transcaucasia.

berries, which are dried, ground, and mixed with a dark, inferior flour that is shipped from the south. White flour is a dainty enjoyed by the wealthiest only, as are also any fruits and vegetables that are imported. The few potatoes grown in the country do not mature, and are of very inferior quality. Hardier vegetables could be grown, but the people undertake nothing their fathers did not do.

Nature has attractions even in Siberia, especially in winter. I could almost be content to live there — in freedom. The country is beautiful. The great firs, bent under their load of snow, seem like gray-haired patriarchs. But the reflection of the sunlight on the snow is so dazzling that it often causes injury to the sight.

CHAPTER VIII

THE "ARRESTED" TESTAMENT

SOON after our arrival in Siberia, we sent home for a Bible; but because of the interruption of traffic at the time of the breaking up of the ice, we had to wait a long time for a response. In the meantime, we learned that there was in the village one Bible, the property of the church. It was in the care of the school-teacher. We asked her to lend it to us; and she did so, on condition that we keep the transaction strictly secret. We had also the Testament that was given us by the warden of the prison at Kursk.

When news spread relative to the unusual character of some of the exiles who had arrived in the village, much wonderment was excited. Many of the people, from curiosity, came to see us, and some became interested in the Bible. Among these latter was a young Polish war prisoner. He ceased to associate with the criminal exiles, and gave evidence of a real desire to become acquainted with the Scriptures.

In those times, we felt assured that the things we had undergone were not without

(115)

benign purpose, and that God had something for us to do on that outer rim of civilization.

The eldest son of our host was the first person to whom our attention was turned as one we might help. He was married, but lived in the home of his parents, in accordance with Russian custom. In the evening, after the rest of the family had gone to sleep, he would slip quietly into our room, which adjoined his own, and listen while we read aloud. He was amazed as he learned of the teachings of Jesus, which he perceived were very unlike those of the priests.

This young man—called Alexander—had forgotten the little he had learned in his boyhood about reading; and we offered to teach him anew. We also gave him our Testament. He was delighted to possess such a treasure; and thereafter, early in the morning and late at night, we could hear him reading aloud in his own room.

The parents were grateful for our efforts in behalf of their son; and they were proud of his ability to read, even stumblingly. They once invited us to their part of the house, to read the Bible to neighbors who were present. Thus our missionary activities seemed to pro-

A RUSSIAN FAMILY

Three generations of a family frequently live under the same roof in Russia, and all respect the commands of the aged grandfather.

ceed smoothly; yet we knew, from former experience, that a conflict with the priest was sure to follow.

Our earnest young pupil was often with us at worship time; and he wondered that we did not bow before the pictures of the saints nor make the sign of the cross. One evening, we read Acts 17:25, which says that God does not require to be "worshiped with men's hands." From that day, Alexander would not make the sign of the cross.

We had not expected such prompt and decided action on his part; and we were fearful that the opposition his course would create, might discourage him. A few mornings later, he told us that his wife had been grieving all night, because she had discovered that he had ceased to wear a crucifix.

Persons unfamiliar with the religious spirit of imperial Russia, will not readily comprehend how seriously this young man's conduct was regarded. That some of the exiles did not show reverence to the symbols of worship of the state church was not considered particularly shocking; but for a member of that church to refuse to do so, caused great excitement.

A TYPICAL PEASANT HOME IN RUSSIA

The yoke on which the wife and mother carries her water buckets — though the men of the household may be idle — is also typical.

The idea of force in religion prevailed there; and the general sentiment was, that all must be compelled to conform to the usages of the church. The priest was king and god.

We counseled our young pupil to act cautiously, on his wife's account; but he asked, in consternation, if we meant that he should do contrary to the Bible teaching. This certainly we did not advise; yet we knew that he was not thoroughly instructed, and we feared that the trial he would surely meet, might be more than he could bear.

The parents, though hitherto they had been friendly toward us, now became quite the reverse, and the father ordered us to leave the premises. We were not obliged to obey this order, as it was not given through the guard.

The son was treated very harshly by his parents. They agreed with the people of the village, that both he and we should be exiled to a more remote part of the country, unless he resumed his former religious observances. Still the young man declared, "Never again will I bow before the icons, or kiss the hand of the priest, since I have learned from the Bible how to pray." Frequently he found opportunity to come to our room for instruction.

When he sought to explain, to those who tried to dissuade him from his course, why he did as he did, they would not listen.

Some urged the father to beat him. Indeed, as the climax of an altercation between the two, the father did strike his son in the face. Alexander had been a person of passionate temper, yet he was calm under this provocation. He said to his father, that in the past, he had not been a good son; he had been so ill-natured to his younger brother as to make it necessary sometimes for the boy to stay away from home. Yet his behavior had not been severely censured; but now that he had turned from his wrong ways, he was denounced and beaten.

One Sunday morning about that time, the priest of the parish visited our little village. In the course of the church services, he made extravagant and groundless accusations against sectarians; and after this tirade, he remarked the presence of some of the proscribed class in the settlement, and charged the people not to allow us in their houses.

As a result of this speech, we doubtless should have met with violence, had we not been under police protection.

That afternoon, as we sat at our frugal dinner, the priest and his assistant, with a crowd of the men of the village, came storming into our room. We greeted them courteously, and invited the priest to be seated; but he indignantly declined, and demanded to see the New Testament we had given to Alexander. He asserted that it was not the same as was used by the Russian church, and he had come to "arrest" it, that it might be sent to the district police, to ascertain whether it was orthodox.

Alexander had gone away some days before on a fishing trip, and had not yet come back. As he always kept his Testament with him, the priest could not get it then; but the father was commanded to go and bring it to him. Although the distance was considerable, the father obediently set out by canoe to secure the offending Testament.

The Bible that we had borrowed from the school-teacher lay on our table when the priest was in the room; but fortunately he did not recognize it, else he might have made trouble for the teacher.

Gorelic opened the Bible, and read therefrom refutations of statements the priest had made in the church. The people present were astounded at Gorelic's boldness in presuming to contradict the assertions of their priest.

Alexander's father, on reaching the place where the son was, told him we had sent for the Testament. Only by such trickery could he have obtained it. The young man, though deeply regretting that we should ask for the return of the treasured gift, yielded it up; but when he came back home, he learned of the deception that had been practiced on him.

We cannot say that this father was not prompted by love for his son. Presumably he believed that the only hope for the young

A Hollow Log Fishing Canoe on a Siberian River

man's salvation lay in his giving up what he had learned from the sacred Scriptures.

A brother-in-law of Alexander's, named Paul, a man of some education, was at their home during this time; and he also studied the Scriptures with us, and became convinced that many of the teachings of the Greek Catholic Church were erroneous. He likewise adapted his mode of worship to his new convictions, and thus incurred the disapproval of his relatives and others; but they did not take such rigorous measures to dissuade him as they had employed with Alexander.

Paul was superintendent of a company of carpenters, and he traveled from place to place, overseeing their work. Wherever he went that season, he spread the story of the strange exiles and their strange religion. Afterwards, as we passed over the same route, we found that a knowledge of our faith had preceded us to every settlement, notwithstanding the limited means for conveying news.

As the parents of Alexander made it impracticable for us to remain in their house, we sought a room elsewhere; but not many of the people of the village dared let us so much as cross their thresholds.

THE "ARRESTED" TESTAMENT 125

One man agreed to let us share a room in his house with an exile who already occupied it, if the latter was willing. Later, when we called to inquire as to this exile's decision, the owner of the house had changed his mind. Possibly he had learned of our identity. Thus we were disappointed in our expectations.

One of the exiles at this station was a wealthy manufacturer, who had obtained permission for his wife to join him there. We were on sociable terms with him; and when he heard of our having thought to take a room with the exile before mentioned, he told us the following story:

Before his wife's arrival, he had lived in a house with this other exile and two or three more; and one night, they extorted from him, by threats and force, a large sum of money. Then they warned him that no mercy would be shown him if he should report what they had done.

Certainly we were thankful that we had not taken one of these unscrupulous characters as a roommate.

The prospects for getting living quarters were discouraging; but in due time, our heavenly Father directed us to a place He had provided for us. We called upon a man who was in ill health and in very straitened circumstances; and when we proposed to rent a part of his house, and laid upon the table before him the few rubles we could pay in advance, he gladly accepted this source of relief from his financial embarrassment.

As we were moving to our new location, the village was startled by the clanging of the bell of the little chapel. A house on the outskirts of the settlement was found to be on fire. As a strong wind was blowing from that direction, the whole village apparently was doomed; for the buildings were close together, there was no provision for fighting fire, and most of the men were away on a fishing tour. The women frantically cried to the pictures of the saints, and even carried these objects of worship to the burning structure, imploring them to put out the fire.

Gorelic and I hurried to the place, and did all we could to save the homes from which we had been excluded. Other exiles also helped.

The stables were connected with the dwellings; and on the roofs of the stables were stacked the remnants of the year's crop of hay. On these high stacks and the grass-thatched roofs of the houses nearest the fire, we stationed some of the people, and had buckets of water passed to them from the stream near, that any spark lighting on the inflammable material might be immediately extinguished.

The burning building, we knew, could not be saved; and with such help as we could get, we tore away the part that was not yet afire, to prevent the flames from getting too strong headway.

A cry was raised that a child was in the burning house. I quickly prepared to make

WEEPING, NOT LAUGHING
The Russians are an emotional people, and sometimes their mourning might be mistaken for laughter.

my way in and rescue the little one; but when I had drenched my clothing with water, and broken a window, preliminary to the attempt, word came that the child was outside.

The only loss was the one building, with the calves and sheep that perished in it.

Soon after the fire was out, some of the men returned from fishing; and men and women gathered about and gazed at us in bewilderment. They could not understand why we whom they had thought to be more dangerous to the community than were the criminal exiles even, should have exerted ourselves as we had done for their sakes.

The result of this incident was a genuine gratitude on the part of the people. Most of them were still distrustful of our religion; but some did not fail to see that the icons in which they had been taught to believe, were powerless to protect even themselves, as those in the burning building had been reduced to ashes.

On the second night in our new room, I was wakened by an exclamation from Gorelic, just as a man was disappearing through a window. There was another man outside, who undoubtedly had been acting as sentinel. He was one of the exiles we had known in prison. Our belongings were scattered about the floor, and the little money we had had was gone.

We gave chase to the intruders, but could not overtake them. Afterwards we learned that the settlers, and even the guards, found it necessary to comply with the thieves' code in the matter of punishing offenders, as there were not enough guardsmen to control them absolutely.

According to that code, if a man was caught stealing, and could be overpowered on the spot, he might be delivered over to the guard, or even punished by his captors, and such a course would be acknowledged as just; but if he got away, then to bring any accusation against him, however strong the proof of his guilt might be, was to call down upon one's self the wrath of the whole "gang."

Several later attempts were made to force an entrance to our room; but after the one experience, we made sure that our doors and windows were well fastened.

The family with whom we had taken up our abode were genial in their attitude toward us; and through their influence, others came to be less suspicious of our religion.

Not infrequently persons came to us to inquire about the Bible. But they came privately; for if they were known to be in sympathy with us, they would be ranked as outcasts, even by their own families.

At one time, as we were walking outside the village, a young man hiding in the tall grass by the roadside accosted us, requesting that we come and talk with him. We did as he asked, and explained to him the fundamentals of the gospel message we proclaim.

At the little shop where we often made purchases, the owner's daughter sometimes waited upon us; and when no one was in hearing, she eagerly asked us about the teachings of the Bible. She wished to know how to pray to Jesus. Her mother, on learning what the daughter was doing, poured out a flood of wrath upon her.

For the sake of those who sought instruction from us, we maintained the utmost secrecy relative to such interviews; but when the parents of this young woman had learned of her having had religious conversations with us, we did not hesitate to risk their greater displeasure by going to them again. Through their love of money, we gained access to them,

A Russian Village Post Office It is also, as shown by the shoe over the door, a cobbler's shop. The priest is distinguished by his garb.

to make purchases; and then we tried to impress upon their minds the truths of Scripture. Some members of the family became to a degree mollified, but others were the more enraged at us.

Again efforts were made to reclaim Alexander to the state church. He was summoned to the government headquarters of the district of Narym — a village of the same name, facetiously called a city — and there he was interrogated in reference to his religion. The priest, finding it impossible to overthrow Alexander's defense, raised a question as to his sanity. But the civil officers allowed the young man to go free. Still he was regarded much as a criminal in his own village.

He was required to leave the parental home; but his wife became in a measure reconciled to his course, and her family also were tolerant toward the "new religion."

CHAPTER IX

A PENAL ISLAND

BY the pressure of the water from the south, the ice was carried away from the point on the Ob where our settlement was located; but as it did not find an outlet at the still frozen mouth of the river, it formed a dam, and the water gradually spread out beyond the banks. The village became completely surrounded by water, and the country was soon flooded as far as we could see.

The fish found more bountiful fare outside the river channel than they had had inside, and became almost too fat to move, whereas they had been very lean before. Men sometimes waded out into the water and caught them in their hands.

With the warm weather came wild ducks in vast flocks. Hunters sold ducks for little more than the traditional price of sparrows.

When, later in the summer, the water receded from the land, there arose from the wet ground clouds of mosquitoes. The air was full of them. They were in eyes, ears, and nostrils.

We obtained permission from our guard to go by boat to a place on the river where we could get some birch saplings, to make a frame over which we could stretch netting to cover our beds at night. In the forest, a worse enemy than the mosquitoes attacked us — myriads of gnats, which actually dimmed the sunlight. We had thought we were insured against their onslaughts, as we wore netting over our faces, and had bound our clothing securely at wrists and ankles. But in spite of these precautions, many of the tiny pests penetrated to our flesh; and such torture did they inflict, that we were ill for days.

The mosquitoes and the gnats rob the people of Siberia of much of the enjoyment of their brief summer. But before the summer is over, relief is likely to come in the form of another calamity. Camp fires left burning by careless hunters and fishermen, often spread to surrounding brush and timber, causing forest fires that burn over hundreds of acres. The smoke is suffocating; but it is not wholly an evil, for it does away with the mosquitoes and the gnats.

When the weather permitted, Gorelic and I spent a portion of the Sabbath in a sequestered place a little distance from the village — a depression in the river bank, with natural seats of earth. Among the few who met with us there for Bible study and worship was the young Polish military prisoner. He expressed the hope that when the war was over, he might return to his own country, and there tell the good tidings of salvation.

One evening, we were called to appear before the chief of our guard. He had not been unfriendly to us up to this time, but now he was quite changed. He read to us a communication from the lieutenant governor of the district, directing that in order to stop our "propaganda," we be transferred to Kolgu-

A FUR HUNTER IN THE BOUNDLESS FORESTS OF SIBERIA

yak. The chief ordered that we be ready to start for that place the next morning.

Reluctantly we put together our "seven possessions"; and at the hour specified, we were at the river's edge. The question came to me as to why we should not have refrained from speaking of religion, and thus have been spared this new trial that had come upon us. The thought of banishment to a still more northerly station was most depressing. But soon I could rejoice again in fellowship with my Master, even in suffering.

In a large canoe, with two guards in charge, we pushed off from the bank, and glided out upon the "back" of the Ob.

As we passed out between the great forests that bordered the river, the silence seemed almost holy. So profound was it that even the sound of a drop of water falling from one of our oars was audible.

That scene of the far north was as if nature would concentrate the charm of an entire year in the short summer. And the mirror-like water, reflecting the beauties of the shore, made them more than twofold. In delight at the romantic view, guards and prisoners united, appearing to forget their relationship.

From the water, there came to us a sound of the dip of oars, although we could see no boat other than our own, nor did the sound of any reach us through the air. Not till about an hour later did we meet the boat of which the river had given us tidings — so far does water transmit sound. The occupants were fishermen, and half drunk.

Before night, we were at Narym, the seat of administration for a large though little inhabited territory. Our guards delivered their papers to the chief of police of the district; and as there was no possibility of our escaping from that isolated spot, we were left to ourselves for the night.

While I kept watch over our baggage, Gorelic went in search of lodgings. He met on the street a young Jewish prisoner of war from Galicia — an intelligent, well educated man — and through him, secured quarters in the house of an aged Jew, who was also a prisoner of war.

This young Jew was from the same city as our former fellow prisoner the imperial councilor; and the next morning, he took us across a branch of the Ob to a small island, where we had the great joy of meeting again that fine-spirited Christian man. He had been sent first to Kolguyak, but later had been removed from there, because the conditions he had to meet were seriously affecting his health. When he learned that we were bound for that place, he was dismayed. We were glad that he was in a more favorable location now; for he was an elderly man, and was not inured to hardship.

At Narym, we met an editor of note, who also was an exile. He averred that he stood for the same principle as we — individual liberty — though he was concerned most with the civil aspects of the subject, and we with the

KATUN RIVER, A TRIBUTARY OF THE OB

religious. This man afterwards escaped from exile, and reached the United States.

Late in the day, we boarded the small steamer that was to take us to Kolguyak, the most northern of the penal stations in western Siberia.

As the boat drifted away, almost noiselessly, with the current, the setting sun was spreading a veil of gold over the evening sky. Flocks of wild ducks floating overhead became lost to sight in the luminous glow, or in the dark green background of firs.

Before entering upon the privations that awaited us, we indulged, on the boat, in the unwonted luxury of an ordinary meal — such a luxury as we had not enjoyed for long months.

During the night, the boat stopped at a number of little villages — mere huddles of fishermen's huts. At each place, the villagers were all at the landing; for a call from one of the small river steamers was an important event in their lonely existence.

The next morning, we reached our destination, an island a mile or two across. The population consisted of a few fishermen and traders, with their families, and about twenty exiles.

During the short Siberian summer, boats occasionally passed this island; and once a month or so, one might stop. But in winter, sleds drawn over the ice by horses were the only means of travel.

We had been told at Narym that the one fit associate we would find among the exiles at Kolguyak was a young Austrian prisoner of war. He had heard of us, and he met us cordially when we arrived.

Other exiles also were very affable and were profuse in offers of assistance. But we recognized some of them as former cell mates, with whom we could not safely mingle; and we knew that to keep clear of them from the first would be easier than to break away from them later. Accordingly, we insistently declined their aid. But one of them refused to be repulsed, and seizing some of our baggage, went with us on our search for a place to live.

We applied at the home of a trader, the most well-to-do man on the island. This man never housed exiles; but the military prisoner and the thief who accompanied us assured him that he need not fear to take us into his home, as we were not criminals. Indeed, the thief gave a very clear statement of our case. He represented himself as having come from Odessa, and having known of us there. As a result of the intercession of these two, we were so fortunate as to get lodgings with this family.

Kolguyak is a desolate spot, not so much because of the natural environment, or even the isolation, though the unbroken forests stretch far on either side; but the most dismal feature of the place is its population — principally criminals and semicivilized Ostyaks. Still, the few Russians there are less ignorant than would be supposed. They are really better informed than many of their countrymen in middle Russia.

So far as religion was concerned, we had more freedom here than at Alatayevo. The priest of the parish lived at a village twenty miles away; and he did not come to Kolguyak often. When he did come, his only errand was to get a supply of the liquor made by women of the island, in defiance of the imperial prohibition issued at the beginning of the war.

On one occasion while we were there, this priest, on leaving the steamer on which he had come, gave whispered directions to a by-

A SIBERIAN GREEK ORTHODOX PRIEST
He bears much resemblance to the one who visited Kolguyak.

stander, who forthwith hastened off on his commission; but he did not so quickly return, and the priest became very nervous, as the boat was to stop only a short time. Not until it was moving away did the messenger reappear. Then he tossed an immense bottle to the priest, who succeeded in catching it; but the stopper flew out, and some of the contents gushed out into the cleric's face and beard. For all his plight, he seemed well pleased with the success of his mission.

Our host and his family were confirmed users of this same brand of liquor — stronger than common vodka; and they gambled also. Yet they were very kind to us.

The house contained only two rooms; and these the family shared not only with Gorelic and me, but with our hostess's sister and the latter's husband.

The thieves continued to inflict their society upon us; but our former acquaintanceship with them made us sure that their object was to get access to the premises, with an eye to plunder. Had we let ourselves be drawn into association with them, we must have forfeited the shelter of the trader's rude home. Instead, we soon won his full confidence.

We sometimes slept out of doors. One night when we had chosen to sleep in the house — for what reason, I do not now remember — thieves forced an entrance into the store, and carried away what money had been left there. The trader never gave the least intimation that he suspected us of being in any way responsible for the raid; and obviously there was no ground for such suspicion, as we could not have left the room where we slept, without stepping over his body.

Here, as at Alatayevo, there were gnats and mosquitoes in such swarms as sometimes to obscure the daylight. It was unsafe to venture away from the settlement without careful protection from these minute pests. They were not so numerous about the dwellings as elsewhere.

CHAPTER X

A FAVOR FROM THE CZAR

WHEN we had been two weeks on the island, the chief of the guard came to us with an official document—the czar's reply to the petition we had sent to the czarina when we were at Kursk.

Six months had passed since the sending of our petition, and I had forgotten the incident. Not till some hours later did I recall it. The experiences of those months had tended to erase many things from my memory.

Our request had been that we be stationed in Ufa, the westernmost district to which exiles were sent. The czar's response was to the effect that if we still wished to go there, the Narym officials should see that we were taken.

Transfer to the city of Ufa, or to that vicinity, would be a great concession; but the district of that name is large, and some parts of it would be even more objectionable than the place where we were. However, we signified our desire to be transferred, and looked forward hopefully to improved conditions.

Then followed weeks and months of suspense before anything further developed in

(145)

reference to the matter. Each time that we heard the signal of an approaching boat, we expectantly looked for orders for our transfer. Repeated disappointments became very disheartening.

In a little open space in the forest, not far from the settlement, stood a solitary tree, beside one that had fallen. To the seclusion of this spot we often went, and there found courage and comfort in prayer. This quiet retreat became very hallowed to us.

The physical discomforts we endured were not so distressing as the lack of freedom, and the loneliness, among the drunken settlers and the still more depraved exiles. We could not so much as go across the river for a half hour without leave from the guard; and we were never allowed to go by ourselves. Yet we were very grateful that we two were permitted to remain together.

When, at intervals of several weeks, a small steamer touched at the island, bringing us intelligence from the distant world — perchance a letter from home — we were almost overwhelmed with emotion.

Even so far north as we were, the heat is sometimes extreme in summer, and the hu-

NICHOLAS II AND HIS FAMILY

midity very oppressive. As we could hardly sleep indoors now, we constructed a small sleeping tent of two sheets, supplemented with thin cotton cloth that we bought for the purpose.

A few bricks formed our cooking range, and the ground answered as chairs and table. Our principal food was fish; but we varied this by the manner of cooking it. At first, we fried it, European style. Afterwards we tried boiling it. Next we adopted the Siberian method, that of baking.

Then we devised a plan for smoking it. By digging in the side of the river bank, we improvised a smokehouse, cutting a chimney through from the surface. The fish that we smoked there was much coveted by the people of the island, who wished us to sell some to them; and we were glad to eke out thus our very scant funds. This enabled us to purchase a little flour, also wild berries that the Ostyaks brought into the settlement for sale; and of the two, we made *vareniki*—a sort of dumpling dear to the palate of a Russian. When a boat came up from the south, we could even give ourselves so rare a treat as a morsel of vegetables.

When we had tired of fish however cooked, we resorted to the natives' custom of salting and drying it. We could eat the dried fish for a longer time and with better relish than that prepared in any other way.

The summer in northern Siberia ends with July, and we did not mourn its close. The cold air of August served us a good turn, in that it did away with the insects.

There are in this part of Siberia remnants of a barbarous tribe called the Tungus, who, unlike the Ostyaks and other tribes, have not yet become at all civilized, but live their nomadic life in the forest.

Often a fire built by some of the Tungus, to roast their bear meat or other game, is left when they move on; and thus forest fires are started, which destroy great amounts of standing timber. The heaviest loss from these fires, to the little Russian settlements, is that of the pine nuts, almost their only source of income. Such fires may rage from springtime till the coming of the autumn snows. No effort is made to check them, except when they endanger a village.

August brought a forest fire to our district —grand, but appalling. The whole region was shrouded in semi-darkness. For a number of days, boats could not make their way on the river. Birds beat about helplessly, unable to find food or home. Wild creatures of

DRYING BEAR SKINS

the wood swam the river to the island, to escape the fire; and fear made them almost as tame as domestic animals.

So choked were we by the smoke, that we wondered whether we should not be smothered to death. But a change in the wind drove the smoke away from us; and river, forest, and sky again appeared, a bright, new world.

That August brought darkness of another sort to me — darkness such as I had never known before. In a Christian home and a

Christian school, I had been instructed in the principles of our faith; and for three or four years, I had been a teacher of these same principles, which I believed implicitly.

But now a procession of strange questions ran through my mind: Why need I suffer banishment, with all its attendant misery, when many good people so shaped their course as not to bring upon themselves such consequences? Instead of persisting in evangelistic work, why could I not give my energies to other employment, in which I would avoid the hardships I now had to meet? Was it possible that our opponents were in the right, after all, and that we were not warranted in our interpretation of the Scriptures?

Though I could repeat from memory abundant Bible texts in support of our faith, yet I was impelled to study them anew from the printed Word, to see if I was after all mistaken. My mind was so harassed, I could not eat or sleep, but hid away in the forest, and there studied and prayed.

The Sabbath had always been a delight to me; and with its return at the close of that week of turmoil, there came such peace and happiness as I had never before known. That penal island seemed a glorified spot. A celestial presence was as real to me as if it had been visible.

Before we were transferred to that station, our minister in Tomsk had written that he intended to visit us; but our being sent farther away prevented the carrying out of his plan. This was a grievous disappointment for us. Now our minds turned to a visit from some one else outside the settlement as a relief from the monotony of our surroundings.

As we were having our morning Bible study together on Sabbath, we espied two strangers passing; and their appearance was so unlike that of the settlers and exiles about us, that we hastened out to meet them. They went inside with us, and we learned that they were connected with a government camp some twenty miles away, where a company of men were getting out railroad ties.

These two had had occasion to go by canoe from their camp to the nearest steamer landing, and on the return trip, had lost their way in the dense smoke, and unintentionally reached our island. They were Mennonites, and as such, were exempt from the bearing of arms, but not from noncombatant military

SCENERY ALONG THE KATUN

duty. Hence it was that they were serving their country in this far section of the earth.

They joined us in our Scripture reading, singing, and prayer. One of the two was a minister, and he was accustomed to conduct religious meetings in their camp. We gave them a small volume of Bible readings that we had, and explained to them some of the distinctive doctrines of our church. When we parted, it was as friends in Christ. A few weeks later, we learned that the minister was presenting to his congregation the subjects we had studied together, and others that were treated in the volume of Bible readings we gave him.

Thus was the smoke of the forest fire made the bearer of a message of cheer to us, and a message of Bible truth from us.

CHAPTER XI

LOOKING TOWARD EUROPE

WE waited two months in vain expectation of an order for our transfer to Ufa. Then, concluding that the matter had been pigeonholed, we decided to send a telegram to Kerensky, the leader of the socialistic faction of the Duma, begging that the imperial decree be carried out.

Of course, there was no telegraph line to our little island, nor was there even a post office nearer than Narym. But by a man who was going to that place by canoe, we sent a letter to the editor in exile there; and he forwarded our message to Kerensky.

One morning in early autumn, we heard the whistle of a river steamer, and hurried to the landing to learn if there was any news for us. A deputy sheriff of the district came ashore, and informed us that we were to go to Narym to attend to our affairs.

We surely were overjoyed. The steamer was to leave in a few minutes, and we could not well go so soon; but we made preparations to start at the first opportunity. We disposed of such of our few belongings as we did not wish to take with us, giving to a sick exile one of the very comfortable beds we had made.

Our host expressed the wish that we might return, when free again, and continue to teach Christianity to his family and others. Some of these people, I believed, would have been susceptible to the influence of the gospel, but for their addiction to the use of vodka.

Unwilling to wait for the next steamer, which might not come for several weeks, and not having sufficient means to hire a canoe to take us to Narym, we arranged to go to Tymsk, a station about twenty miles below ours, with an islander who was planning to go there in a small boat. Steamers called at that point oftener than at our island.

The time of starting was late afternoon. I was amazed at the beauty of the sunset on the Ob that evening. I have no remembrance of having ever beheld a view more wondrously lovely. A light breeze stirred the surface of the water; and as the sun sank below the dark green rim of the forest, sky and river vied with each other in brilliance.

With darkness came cold creeping upon us from the shore. The breeze died away, and our sails — made of grain sacks — flapped idly.

A pair of oars was brought into use, but erelong one of them broke. Still it was made to do service, and we kept slowly on.

As we passed close along the bank, we saw a big grouse almost within arm's reach. None of our boat's company having brought a gun, the great fowl was in no danger.

A SIBERIAN FAMILY

At a fisherman's hut farther on, our oarsmen — two exiled thieves — wished to stop and rest. There fifteen or twenty men, rough looking but seemingly well disposed, and unmistakably jolly, invited us to have supper with them. We had brought food with us, but we were not averse to a warm place in which to eat, although the tobacco smoke was so thick as to be almost solid.

The little village of Tymsk, being built in the edge of the forest, cannot be seen from the river, even in daylight. Yet we were in no doubt as to its location, though we approached it at about midnight; for a watch fire was burning on the bank. The watchman proved to be a Tartar exile from my native Caucasus. We enjoyed the warmth of the fire, for the night was cold.

The young Austrian prisoner of war who was our only associate for some time after we went to Kolguyak, had been transferred later to Tymsk; and he had urged that if we should ever come to that station, we stay with him. This invitation we now accepted.

His boarding place was the home of the village lay assistant to the drunken priest we had sometimes seen at Kolguyak. This assistant evinced real interest in our religion, and remarked that there was too much commercialism in the state church.

The next morning, we met a man who had been banished on the ground that he spoke German to employees in his mill, though he declared that he did not speak German, but the Dutch dialect generally used by the Mennonites, they having come originally from the Netherlands.

Late in the evening of that day, a stampede of every person in the settlement in the direction of the landing, heralded the coming of a steamer. As I realized that this boat was to take me from the scene of my banishment, my feelings were such as I shall not try to put into words.

The little steamer was northbound, and would go as far as Kolguyak, but would not call at Tymsk on the return voyage. Thus we were obliged to go back to the island. But we stayed there only an hour, then started for Narym.

This boat brought us mail that had been sent months before. Among it was my Bible. My joy at receipt of the precious volume was unbounded.

There were two Chinese silk traders on the steamer, one of whom entertained us with Chinese singing. I had never before seen chopsticks used, and I did not imagine that soon I should make use of such myself.

When we reached Narym, the exiled editor was the first to greet us. He had been influential in having the deputy sheriff send for us; for he was on fraternal footing with the sheriff, although one was an officer of the law, and the other an offender against it.

We again saw the imperial councilor, with whom our association had been so congenial, notwithstanding the difference between us in nationality, station, and age. One of his keenest trials here was lack of agreeable associates.

At police headquarters, we learned that as a result of the sending of our telegram to Kerensky, word had come that we should be permitted to go immediately to Ufa, without convoy.

Navigation would close soon. A boat was to leave for the south that night; and a man was sent by canoe to notify the Baptist ministers still at Alatayevo, that they were at liberty to start by that boat for European

Tiflis, Capital of Transcaucasia

Russia. They arrived at Narym in time, and proceeded south; but Gorelic and I, for some incomprehensible reason, went to sleep, and did not wake up till the boat had gone. Another boat came the next day, though, and that we did not fail to board.

Before leaving Narym, we met the Polish exile whom we had known at Alatayevo. At his request, I had ordered a Polish Bible for him, which he had since received; and he read it with great satisfaction.

When our steamer stopped at Kalpasheva, we caught sight of one of our ministers, A. Osol, in the crowd on shore, and had a few minutes' visit with him. He had been arrested at Tiflis, capital of Transcaucasia, and banished to this station. His jail ordeal had been worse than ours.

This minister, when a young man attending missionary training school, had been instructed in the care of the sick; and now his knowledge in that line was put to excellent use. Hundreds of the people applied to him for aid, and he worked hard to help them. About a year later, this good man died of typhus fever, caused, undoubtedly, by conditions he had encountered in prison.

Our little steamer made better time than the one our friends were on, and we reached Tomsk before they did. The next morning, we made application for our safe conducts to Ufa, at the office of the lieutenant governor of Narym, who lived at Tomsk.

There we met the rest of our company. Among them was the Baptist minister who, after we had left the last jail on our way into exile, about seven months before, was sent back to Odessa for trial on an additional charge brought against him by members of "the Black Society." Had that charge been proved, the penalty would have been two years in one of the horrible Russian jails — if death did not occur before that time had elapsed. He was cleared of the charge, but then he was returned to Siberia on the former sentence, and arrived at our first place of exile after we had been removed to the island station.

Before the hour appointed for us to start for Ufa, Gorelic and I sought out our minister at Tomsk. We were surprised to see, over the chapel door, a sign announcing the services. All our meeting places in Russia had been closed soon after the war began; but in

Siberia, the land of exile, there was more freedom for those not exiles, than there was in Russia.

In a very happy mood we made the journey of three or four days to Ufa. We were coming closer to the world from which we had been so far separated. Instead of being transported by *étape*, we traveled by regular passenger train, with no guards to watch us.

When we reported to the governor, he commanded that we leave the city at once. The German Baptist was to go in one direction, another of the Baptists and I to the little city of Birsk, about a hundred miles distant, and Gorelic and the rest to a third place. The governor would not listen to any plea for a reconsideration of his decision.

At Birsk, I was encouraged at the prospect of a not uncongenial abode. I secured a pleasant room in the home of a family whose son was a prisoner of war in Germany. They said that I resembled him; and from their bearing toward me, one might have judged that I was really he.

As was customary, I must call at the police station each morning. In ten days, there came to the police a communication from the

RAILWAY STATION AT OMSK
In Siberia, some of the best buildings are those of the railway.

governor, directing that I be transferred to a village on the Tartar steppes. Evidently the governor had set his face to make our lot harder than it had been in Siberia.

From Tomsk, I had written to our mission treasurer; and the day before I was to leave Birsk, a reply came, and with it some money. The amount was much more than an exile ordinarily was allowed to have; but after some delay, it was delivered to me. With it I purchased such articles as I most needed.

The hour for me to start for my destination had come. My companion in exile had already gone to his station. I had my "wolf's passport"— a passport that does not give the bearer a right to go anywhere except to the point named, nor to tarry by the way, save to eat and to sleep.

I was to travel without a "black angel"— that is, a guard— and had one week in which to make the journey and appear before the police at its end. My baggage was packed, and the man I had engaged to take me by wagon was already overdue. As I waited impatiently for him, a strange thought surprised me— one which I had meager time to act upon or even to develop.

HIDE MARKET OF KAZAN TARTARS

I had been told that the last steamer of the season would go to Ufa that night. Why should I not board it, and endeavor to escape exile? The thought of spending an indefinite period on the cold, wild steppes of the Kazan Tartars, naturally was not attractive to me. With a rush of thought, my course was outlined. It was a hazardous one; and in case of recapture, my punishment would be such as I dared not think of.

There was no time to deliberate; but I uttered a brief prayer that I might be kept from starting upon the project unless I could carry it through.

The chief of police himself had left the door of escape ajar for me. When the Baptist who had been with me here went to the police station to say that he was ready to start for the place to which he had been assigned, the officer inquired when I intended to leave; and being told that I was preparing to go the same day, he said that I need not come to notify him, as my comrade's statement would suffice.

Had I myself told the police that I was about to start for the Tartar territory, I would not have violated my word; but as the extraordinary lenity of the chief left me uncommitted, I did not feel that to evade the authorities would be dishonorable. The question was as to my being able to do so.

During the week that I was supposed to be on the road, I would be comparatively free from police surveillance. Even for several days more, my nonarrival might be attributed to some mishap. Thus I should have time to go a long distance before my escape was suspected, if I could but get away from Birsk, where I was known to the police.

I said to my host, that as the man I had hired to take me had not come, I should go by boat. I did not tell him that the place to which I now designed to go was not a place of banishment, but my parents' home in far southern Russia; and he apparently was not aware that no boat was scheduled to leave Birsk at that time, that would take me to the Tartar country.

My first danger lay in the fact that the steamer agent to whom I must apply for a ticket, was, like all men in similar position in Russia in war time, a sort of government detective. If I should elude his vigilance, I must pass between two lines of policemen in crossing the gangplank to board the steamer. I took my baggage to the steamer station, which was only a few blocks away, then went back to my room, where I stayed till near the time for the steamer to go.

How, I wondered, could I pass that double row of policemen? One plan occurred to my mind; but it might seem like an imposition on the fatherly spirit my host had manifested toward me. It was this: The two daughters of the family, being students in the gymnasium, wore the dress peculiar to such; and any one seeing them on the street with a young man, would take for granted that he was a brother or other relative, or at least a fellow student. So I suggested to the parents that the daughters accompany me to the steamer; and ready assent was given to this proposition.

At the ticket window, a crowd of people awaited their turn. The agent noticed me as I entered the waiting room; and motioning the others to stand aside, he inquired what I wanted. This seemed to me like a challenge, but I simply replied that I wished a ticket to Ufa. He handed me a ticket, then asked whether I would like a private stateroom. As a safeguard against observation, a private

OLD-TIME FARMING METHODS
Haymaking affords pleasure as well as employment for both men and women in Russia.

stateroom certainly would be desirable; and I answered that I would take one. Receiving the key, I left the room, the first menace to my dangerous undertaking safely passed.

Why I was treated as if I were a dignitary, I do not know. True, my clothing was of good quality; and my eyeglasses, with black ribbon attached, were such as were not commonly worn in that part of Russia except by scholarly people. Yet I must believe that more than natural influences were exercised in my behalf.

CHAPTER XII

A "WOLF'S PASSPORT"

BETWEEN my fair young guardians—who were wholly unaware of their office—I crossed the gangplank, chatting busily, as if quite unobservant of surroundings; although I certainly was not forgetful of the policemen ranged along either side. On deck, we continued our ostensibly merry conversation until the whistle gave warning of the steamer's departure; but I was careful to stand where I was not conspicuous.

As the unsuspecting misses, having returned to the wharf, saw the steamer head toward Ufa instead of in the opposite direction, their faces told that they were puzzled; but I waved them a reassuring good-by, then went into my stateroom.

Scarcely ten minutes passed before there was a rap at my door; and when I opened it, the purser stood before me. He asked to see my ticket. His request would have caused me no concern, but that the Russian word he used for ticket was one that is sometimes used to indicate a passport. In my confusion, I produced my "wolf's passport." The purser, after glancing at it, questioned whether it entitled me to free transportation.

I understood, then, that he had meant to call for my ticket; and I handed it to him, which was all he required. He may not have observed that the place designated in my "wolf's passport" was one we were leaving farther behind us each moment; or perhaps he surmised my intentions, but was not disposed to hinder me.

The next morning, we arrived at Ufa. I almost expected that officers would be waiting at the wharf to apprehend me; but I was not molested. I went direct to the railway station. To my chagrin, I learned that no train would leave for the west till late in the afternoon. Putting my baggage in a corner of the waiting room, I concealed myself in the manner that I believed to be most effectual; that is, walking boldly about the streets. This I did till time to board the train.

I bought a ticket for Samara, whence I thought to travel by boat to Tsaritsyn. To lessen expense, I would have traveled third-class, except for the greater privacy afforded by the second-class coaches. In these, a person could have a compartment to himself, and shut himself in, if there were not too many passengers; but the third-class coaches were not divided into compartments. I refrained from leaving the train at stations, as to be seen by any of the gendarmes on duty there might be disastrous for me.

I reached Samara the next morning, but had not quite enough money to pay my passage on the steamer to Tsaritsyn. It was at Samara that a minister of our church had visited me in jail when I was on the way to Siberia, and I now determined to hunt him up; but the city is a large one, and I did not know what part of it he lived in. When persistent inquiry for him and for our church brought no reward, I decided to find, if possible, a church of some of the other sects, as I might in that way learn of the whereabouts of our own.

I met an old woman carrying a basket of vegetables, and I asked her if she knew where the Baptist church was. She did not; but she pointed to a chapel near, which she said belonged to another sect. It was our very own! In connection with this building was the home of the minister I sought, whose visit to Gorelic and me in jail had been so great a comfort to us. He and his family received me hospitably; and the little time spent with them was a season of refreshment to me, spiritually and physically. He lent me the few rubles lacking to pay my passage on the steamer — which amount I sent back to him a few days later.

On a better steamer than I had thought to see in that part of the country, I proceeded down the Volga. "Mother Volga" this river is called, as it has its source in the region where the Russian nation was cradled.

I felt more secure on the boat than on land. I had a stateroom alone; and though nearly

ON THE VOLGA

two days on board, I hardly spoke with one person. Indeed, there were few passengers, as travel on the Volga is limited chiefly to summer, when many pleasure seekers make the long journey down to the Caspian Sea.

During those early October days, the clouds were dark and foreboding, as was the outlook before me. Still I was grateful to the Father who had brought me thus far.

On the second night, we reached Saratov, where the steamer was to stop a number of hours. Our denominational headquarters for all of Russia were then located in Saratov. I went ashore in search of them; and having the address, I succeeded in finding the place.

There I learned that the work of the mission was advancing, though many of our workers had been exiled, and others had been called into the army.

Before leaving to go back to the steamer, I drew most of the money the mission held to my credit. This would meet the expense of the rest of my journey homeward, and also repay the amount borrowed of our minister at Samara.

After another day of slow travel by boat, I landed at Tsaritsyn. To avoid the distressing self-consciousness that I could not easily throw off when alone, I made companions of two Armenians who had been with the army in the Caucasus.

Two more days by train took me, utterly intoxicated with joy, to the town of my birth, where most of my relatives lived. My parents' home was a little farther on.

At the station, I pulled my cap low over my face, and thought that sufficient precaution against detection, as I did not suppose I should be readily recognized after having been absent for years. Indeed, so free did I feel, away from all the reminders of exile, that I did not fully sense the need of caution.

As I was leaving the station, I met an old man, who addressed me by name. I was in consternation. This might mean that I should be cast back into Dante's inferno just when I was about to enter Paradise.

The delight of my relatives on my appearance at the old homestead, was eclipsed by grief when they learned that I came to them a refugee. As for myself, I was weary in body and in spirit. My sweet aged grandmother perceived this; and after a time, she took me authoritatively by the arm — though

MOUNT USHBA, IN THE CAUCASUS RANGE — NEARLY AS HIGH AS PIKES PEAK

she was a wee body in comparison with my six feet one — led me to her quiet apartments, and left me there to sleep.

It is said of the disciples of Christ, that as they waited for Jesus in Gethsemane, they slept "for sorrow." (Luke 22:45.) I slept in the ancestral home, whether "for sorrow" or from exhaustion, or both.

I woke at the sound of footsteps in the hallway. One of our ministers who was in the village at the time, had come, by request of my uncle and grandmother, to consider with me plans for my future. Behind locked doors, we discussed the question.

To remain in the home of my relatives would jeopardize not only my own safety, but also theirs, and even that of the church. The course I had had in mind from the first — that of seeking concealment with a friend who lived in the foothills not far away — was declared to be impracticable. The suggestion was made that I cross the Caspian into Persia; but I had no ear for such a scheme, as I knew of the revolutionary spirit prevalent in Persia, the taking over of control of that country by Russia, and Turkish invasions of the territory.

With an air of conviction, the venerable man told me to make a note of the following names: Irkutsk, Harbin, Mukden, Shanghai, San Francisco. Those five cities, he affirmed, should mark my route.

Our interview was not long. It closed with earnest prayer. The expression of confidence on the good minister's face, and the prayer he uttered, seemed to raise my mind above all misgivings, and I unhesitatingly accepted his counsel, though it might appear impossible of execution.

I must see my father and mother before starting on this long and venturesome journey. First I went to the home of a friend a few miles from their home; and thence, in the evening, he walked with me over the fields and the hills to the town where my parents lived. At a little bridge near their home, I lingered behind, in order that he might announce my coming; for I feared that to see me unexpectedly would be too great a shock to my delicate mother.

My parents were more startled than rejoiced at my coming. Father could speak but a few words, and mother seemed unable to fathom the mystery of my presence.

182 ESCAPE FROM SIBERIAN EXILE

There were wearisome days and nights behind me, and I looked forward to similar ones to come. Therefore I begged that we sleep as much as we could that night, specially as the subjects we should be most likely to talk upon were painful ones to us all. Accordingly, with the benediction of my father's prayer, we went to our rest.

CHAPTER XIII

THE BEGINNING OF A PERILOUS JOURNEY

BEFORE the first sign of dawn, we were all astir; for I must leave ere the day should betray me. My mother's heart evidently was crushed with grief. If my family could have had any assurance that I should accomplish even so much as a tenth of the proposed journey, they would have had hope in reference to the remainder; but I might not even be permitted to leave the first station, and to be detected would imply a fate far worse than death.

My success in evading capture hitherto, was no proof that I should not be seized by the next gendarme I met — except as it denoted the protection of One against whom all the minions of the czar could not prevail.

The farewell was agonizing. My father led the way through the garden, and to a footpath along the bank of the Kuma. Then, with the friend who had come with me, I passed out into the darkness. Equally dark my future loomed. Yet I faced it with hopefulness and even enthusiasm.

Though we kept as far as practicable from public roads and human habitations, we necessarily went near a little village; and the dogs bayed at us with a noisiness that was no aid to secrecy.

The morning had barely conquered the night, when we arrived at the friend's home. I spent the day in hiding there, intending to take an evening train back in the direction from which I had fled.

I did not dare examine the contents of my purse, for my short stay with my family had not given them opportunity to get more for me than they had on hand; but I knew that I had enough to buy a ticket to Irkutsk, about four thousand miles away. To ask for one to take me farther would be to arouse suspicion; for Irkutsk is not a great distance from the frontier, and any man between eighteen and forty-five years of age was forbidden to leave the country in time of war.

When I called for a ticket, the agent's face seemed to ask, "How is this, young man?" But he raised no objection. As the train bore me away, I was glad to see the lights of the station vanish behind me. Each danger passed was a cause of rejoicing, al-

A Railroad Bridge That the Author Crossed, Near Ufa
It was blown up in the recent civil strife.

though new dangers awaited me just ahead. I had not been long on the train when it stopped — for what reason, I did not know. Soon a gendarme, lantern in hand, and accompanied by a subordinate, came into the compartment I occupied. He looked about, then came to me, and ordered his subordinate to search my baggage. This being done, he raised his lantern to my face, held it there for several minutes — so it seemed to me — turned and left the car, and the train moved on.

I cannot explain this incident, except as I explain to my own heart many incidents of that journey — on the supposition that divine power interposed to ward off harm.

My route lay through Ufa, the first town at which I had stopped on my flight. That locality might reasonably be regarded as particularly unsafe for me, and I kept very unobtrusively to my corner. After crossing the Ural Mountains into Siberia, I felt less apprehensive.

Although, in temperate climates, this was the season of reddening leaves and harvest ingathering, winter had already begun in Siberia. The country was covered with snow, and glistening with frost.

After eight days of continuous travel, I was nearing Irkutsk. The question as to how I should be able to go on from there, was still unanswered. Even had I had enough money, I could not have bought a ticket to cross the border. Moreover, where nearly every young man was in military uniform, my civilian garb must attract undesired attention. Then, too, I had no passport; and even before the war, hundreds of times had I been required to show my passport.

A wounded military engineer tried repeatedly to engage me in conversation, and I could not well repulse him altogether. He may have guessed my dilemma; for though no allusion was made to it, after a while, he offered to sell me his uniform and his railway pass. He, being wounded, and having his discharge, could travel in citizen's attire without difficulty; and he could renew his pass in any large city. The one he wished to sell me was for Vladivostok; and to reach that place, the railway crosses Manchuria. Thus the pass would take me over the boundary line.

Was this young soldier actuated by pity for me? Or was his purpose only mercenary — to get the few rubles he asked of me? Or would he lead me into a trap, and then deliver me up to arrest? I did not fear to trust him, and assented to his proposition.

The safest place to conclude our arrangements, I thought, would be the home of our minister in Irkutsk. I had his address; and when we arrived at that city, we took a sleigh —there were many such for hire at the station—and the small Siberian horse that drew it, galloped wildly away.

CHAPTER XIV

IN DISGUISE

THAT there should be more religious liberty in Siberia, the land of exile, than in imperial Russia proper, which pretended to allow its subjects freedom of conscience, was strange; but that such was the case, I was reminded by the sign on the residence of the minister we sought, and on the chapel where he presided—simply an announcement of the services. Such a sign could not have been seen in all Russia, on a building used by members of a "sect."

As the minister was not at home, I briefly told his wife of my errand. She became much perturbed; but I did not think that remarkable, considering how dangerous was the undertaking to which she was asked to become a party. Then she informed us that there was a police officer in an adjoining room. I shall not say that I was undisturbed at the news. Our hostess explained that the officer was there to get details in reference to her son, a young man of military age, who was attending one of our missionary training schools in western Europe.

My soldier companion and I quickly decided to go away for a while, and return after the officer had gone.

We had passed only the first crossing, when out from the crowd emerged a familiar figure —the former superintendent of our Caucasian Mission. He also was a victim of the malice of "Orthodox" priests, and had been exiled to this city. He was not imprisoned, but must report daily to the guard, as must all exiles. I made an appointment to meet him later at the parsonage from which I had just come. Then we separated, for the ever needful purpose of avoiding observation.

We met again as agreed. Our hostess and the superintendent regarded my project as a very daring one. Yet, as they could suggest no other, they gave me such encouragement as they could.

When the exchange of clothing between the soldier and me had been effected, he returned with me to the station, pointed out the train for wounded soldiers which was to leave for Vladivostok that night, and left me.

I began to feel concerned because of having no appearance of being wounded. I had discovered in my baggage a strip of white

VLADIVOSTOK, SIBERIA, EASTERN TERMINUS OF THE SIBERIAN RAILWAY

muslin, which doubtless some member of my family had put there. The one who did so, did better than she knew. I found a place where I could not be seen, and made of the muslin a sling for my right arm. This would not only afford an apparent reason for my being on the disabled soldiers' train, but it would also exempt me from the military requirements relative to saluting, and thus from much exacting scrutiny.

I had to wait two hours at the station. I was an object of some suspicion, or else I interpreted mere curiosity as suspicion. Be that as it may, I affected, as best I could, a forbidding sternness, and boldly paced the platform.

When the first signal was given for the departure of our train, a crowd of wounded soldiers began to gather. Some of them had but one arm, others only one leg, while still others were wounded in various ways.

As is common in Russia, there was much crowding and jostling in boarding the train. I could not manage my luggage very well with my one free hand. When finally I was seated, the soldiers in the same car began to assail me with questions as to what regiment

I was of, what battles I had been in, how I had been hurt, and many other particulars.

I had not expected such a fusillade, and was unprepared for it. Any attempt to answer must have involved me in endless embarrassments. Instantly I bethought myself

RAILWAY STATION AT IRKUTSK

to feign deafness. This was not an easy thing to do without a moment's forethought. Still, my questioners became convinced that I had lost my hearing, and perhaps also my mind to some extent. A few tried speaking loudly to me, even shouting in my ears; but they soon wearied of such efforts. There was speculation among them as to the probable cause of my condition — shell shock, exposure, or what.

A man of middle age, who was in the same compartment as I, assumed a paternal guardianship over me, and prevented others from annoying me with attempts at conversation. He himself communicated to me, largely by signs, any information he thought might be of value to me.

When the conductor came into our compartment, I gave no intimation, at first, that I saw him; but my self-appointed guardian acted as spokesman for me. I had been uneasy over the question of whether my pass would be accepted, or instead, would get me into trouble; and when the conductor marked it and returned it to me without hesitancy, I felt like shouting for joy. Had the fact become known that although wearing a military uniform, I was not a soldier, the consequences would have been such as I was loath to contemplate.

Next morning, our train began to crawl sluggishly up the mountains on the southeast side of the renowned Lake Baikal, whose waters are nearly a mile deep. At the time when the railroad was under construction, it is said, temporary tracks were laid on the ice, and heavy trains run over them.

Boating on Lake Baikal

The country in that vicinity is exceptionally beautiful, contrasting strongly with the dreary steppes over which we had come.

About noon of the first day after we left Irkutsk, as we stopped at a station, "Sisters of Mercy" appeared, and led us to an eating room maintained for disabled soldiers. There long tables were spread with food, principally soup and bread.

The "sisters" were very attentive to us; and after I had finished my meal, some of them volunteered to rebandage my arm. I declined their aid, but one was persistent. She wished to take me to a surgeon in the hospital booth. I was becoming solicitous as to how I could get away from her, for discovery that my arm was not injured would be sure to lead to grave developments.

At that juncture, the engine whistle gave warning that the train was about to start. It was a joyous sound to me. I still had time to obtain some cotton batting, and with it I thoroughly plugged my ears. This made the role of deaf soldier easier, as I then really could not hear much.

The practice of such deception was not pleasing to me, nor was it inspired in any degree by love of adventure, but only by the hope of thus procuring freedom from the tyranny of a despotic government.

At another station where we stopped, I saw in a bookstand a copy of the works of the Caucasian poet Lermantov. As his home had been near my own, his writings had a double charm for me; and I purchased the book, and read from it on the train. That volume of Russian verse afterwards played a part I did not plan when I bought it.

Three days of travel brought us almost to the Chinese frontier, the next critical point in my journey. I had thought that if we reached the frontier at night, I might leave the train and cross afoot unseen; but it was midday when we drew near the line, and to pass the border police unobserved would be impossible. Besides this, when the train approached a station, the doors were locked, and they remained thus until we were well under way again.

I had come to the limit of my resources. In fact, my success thus far was not attributable to any shrewdness on my part. At times when my actions had been such as to avert suspicion, they were not premeditated, but were prompted by an impulse of the moment. Now my frightened heart could only call out to Him who had kept me hitherto.

Gendarmes came on board to examine the passengers. I heard the clank of their sabers. Unless Heaven should interfere, I should never again know freedom. Still, I believed that I should soon be with friends in Harbin, although I had no conception how this could be.

Two of the officers came to my compartment, and one of them brusquely demanded my papers. In the right-hand pocket of my trousers was my railway pass. I knew that it would be of no use to me now; yet, as it was the only military paper I had, involuntarily I reached for it. My right arm being bound up, I essayed to thrust my left hand into my right-hand pocket. The gendarme put a stop to my awkward endeavor by saying that badly wounded soldiers need not present their papers. Then he went on to the next compartment.

I was dumfounded. There had been passing before my mental vision pictures of lifelong imprisonment, with all its agony and torture. Now I could scarcely comprehend

Railway Station at the Boundary Between Siberia and Manchuria

that I had escaped the fate which, only a few moments before, had appeared to be inevitable.

The next town at which we stopped was Manchuria, the first station in the province of the same name. I was much elated at having passed the most dreaded ordeal of all, the crossing of the frontier.

Our train went no farther; but with the few soldiers who had not left it before we reached the border, I was transferred to another train. They were to continue across Manchuria and into Russian territory again. I did not intend to do so, but hoped to escape from the train at Harbin, about two thirds of the distance across.

Over the door of the compartment that I occupied on the new train, was a sign which indicated that the occupants were wounded soldiers. Gendarmes going through the train, saw the sign, and merely glancing into the compartment, went on without calling for our papers. Thus another peril was passed.

The journey through Manchuria furnished scenes new to me. With real enjoyment I watched them from my window. The dark shadow that had hung over my road to freedom was now largely dissipated, and notwithstanding difficulties that I knew I must yet meet, I felt wonderfully light-hearted. Had I known all that was still before me, I should hardly have had courage to face it.

Late in the evening of an early November day — the fifth since we left Irkutsk — our train arrived at Harbin. A horde of vehicle drivers, mostly Manchurians, beset the passengers as they alighted; and I hastily put my luggage into an empty carriage, thinking that in the confusion, I might get away without being seen by the guard. Straightway one of them accosted me, asking why I was leaving the train. I answered that I wished to stop a short time in the city; but he showed no inclination to let me go.

His attention was diverted for a moment; and seizing my baggage, I dashed away into the night and the fog. When I had gone a few yards, I came upon an unoccupied public carriage. Into this I threw my luggage, and signaled the driver to hurry away.

I had the address of our Harbin mission, but could not make the Manchurian cabman understand it. The only course left to me was to make inquiry of some one, though I knew that in so doing, I might leave behind me a clue that would lead to my capture. But no alternative was left me.

The pedestrian of whom I inquired, directed me to the street I wished to find, and the cabman took me to it; but when I reached the house, I learned that our mission had moved. Where it was then located, the new tenant did not know.

There was apparently no way of finding the location, without exposing myself to too much publicity. Even to be on the streets at such an hour, was to attract the notice of the police. I reëntered the carriage, not knowing

A Mountain Road in the Altai Region

what else to do, and ordered the driver to go ahead, although I could not tell him where to go.

Soon I saw a boy of ten or twelve years walking along the street, and I felt impelled to ask him if he knew of any Seventh-day Adventists in the city. He replied that his family were such. This surely was an astounding coincidence, as there were but few of our people in Harbin, and there were few persons on the street that dark, rainy night.

I took the boy into the cab, and he guided me to his home. The father was in prison because of his religious activities. The mother and the other children were alarmed at the appearance of a soldier — which, of course, they took me to be — in their home at that hour; nor were they reassured when I impulsively threw aside the sling that had bound my arm, exclaiming that I had masqueraded long enough. The sense of security that I felt at being among those who I knew would not report me to Russian officials, naturally caused a reaction from the tense secretiveness of weeks past.

My explanation half dispelled the fears of the family, yet I overheard the mother saying to the elder son that he had better go for Mr. Gardishar. I was surprised to hear the name, for it was that of a former schoolmate of mine, and I so stated to the good woman. In response to the message sent him, he hastened to meet me; and his greeting left no distrust in the mind of my involuntary hostess. Her hospitality thereafter was wholly voluntary and cordial.

I gladly put off my military uniform, with its lying epaulets, and donned my accustomed clothing.

More than formal thanks were offered to Heaven that night for my deliverance from danger. Then I slept in peace, although to the charges previously held against me by the czar's government was now added that of desertion.

CHAPTER XV

HIDING

HARBIN, being a Russian city, but on foreign soil, was policed even more strictly than were the cities of Russia. In the hotels, a newcomer was asked to show his passport before taking off his overcoat. Residents were forbidden to harbor any person for one night even, without first notifying the police; and failure to comply with this requirement made the offender liable to any consequences that might befall his guest.

Under these circumstances, the hospitality accorded me by our people in Harbin meant much both to them and to me. Those who lived in rented quarters must keep the owners of the premises in ignorance of my presence, unless these could be trusted not to divulge it, and were willing to risk the results.

The morning after my arrival in the city, I was invited to the home of our former pastor there, and was told that the owner of the house had consented to my coming — a consideration not to have been expected of a stranger, in view of the responsibility involved. The pastor himself was in prison because of his labors in connection with a church that was not indorsed by imperial Russia.

As far as practicable, I avoided being seen by others than our own people. Of some of the latter, I asked counsel in reference to my future course; for how to get out of Harbin was as perplexing a question as had been that of getting in. The railroad was Russian, and therefore not to be considered. Whatever other method of travel I might choose, I should be almost certain of arrest at the bridge I must cross in leaving the city, if I succeeded in getting even so far; and to come into contact with the police meant for me shackles and a dark dungeon.

One of the friends told of a man who some time before had aided several persons to leave Harbin; and it was proposed that his help be sought in my behalf. I caught at this straw, and one of our number was delegated to consult with the man.

The securing of a passport was the main object. To attempt this by irregular means was not regarded by the subjects of old Russia as it would be by loyal citizens of a free government. Yet, I would not have agreed to such a scheme, if I had had the confidence

Doctor Attending an Exile Who Has Fainted Under the Knout

which I should have had in Him who had already brought me out of straits from which no human trickery could have rescued me.

The man to whom I now looked for aid was a Swiss, the Harbin representative of a large foreign shipping company and of other important business interests. When I was introduced to him, he manifested a desire to help me, but said he had better turn the matter over to a Polander in his employ, a political exile.

This Polander was much less prepossessing than his employer. Still, he claimed to be able to get a passport for me, and urged that I accompany him to see the police officer with whom he should have to deal. This I did not think a safe thing to do, but I did advance some money to him, which was declared to be needful.

Day after day I must have tiresome interviews with this fellow, he promising, each time, that I should soon have the desired document, and making a pretense of explaining why he did not yet get it. There were also repeated requisitions for money.

I was disposed to cease the negotiations altogether; but friends advised that I defer such action for a time at least. We looked upon the Swiss as the responsible agent in the transaction; and his position with respectable business concerns, added to his appearance of sincerity, offset in part the unfavorable impression made by his "pool fellow."

In the meantime, another plan was suggested. One of our church people told of a Manchurian who might act as a guide to take me on my way by horseback. This man was brought to me. He was shrewd looking, and knew the country well; but he was not one I should have trusted, except for the assurance of friends.

However, I was persuaded not yet to give up the effort to get a passport, that I might travel by train.

Eventually I seemed compelled to yield to the importuning of the Polander, that I go with him to see the police officer with whom he was treating. My signature was said to be the only thing lacking to obtain the passport.

While we were going to the office, the old trickster presumed to coach me on the answers I should give to questions that might be put to me. As I would not resort to falsehood, his coaching was superfluous.

I was admitted to the presence of the officer I had come to see, the Polander being left waiting in an anteroom. This officer informed me that he understood I had lost my passport; but he said that before he could issue a new one for me, he must telegraph to my home address, in order to verify my statements as to name, place of residence, and so forth.

I knew that such a message sent to the police authorities in my native district would mean my apprehension as an escaped exile. I was in dismay, suspecting that I had been

Street Scene in Harbin, Manchuria, Where Russians and Manchurians Alike Are at Home

betrayed to the police, and that they simply thought to extort more money from me, or to work up their case against me more fully, before letting me know their purpose. I wondered whether I should even be permitted to leave the room, except as a prisoner.

At this stage in the proceedings, another officer came in, looked me up and down, then went out. Still I tried to preserve a semblance, at least, of composure. I said to the officer with whom I had been speaking, that I hesitated to assent to the delay of telegraphing, as a reply might be long in coming, but that I would take a little time to think what I had best do. Then I decorously but quickly left the room.

In entering the building, I had passed through four doorways, each of which was guarded. Had I now believed that I should be allowed to pass out alone, I should have endeavored to evade my uncongenial companion, and get away from him altogether; but it seemed more feasible to let him go with me to the street, and rid myself of him as soon as I could afterwards.

When out of doors once more, I felt as if I had just emerged from a prison. But the

Polander tenaciously kept with me. We were still together when we met an officer of the secret police. Undoubtedly the company I was in was sufficient to mark me as a suspicious character; and without any questioning, the officer bade me go with him. The old man protested, perhaps because he was unwilling to give up hope of wringing the very dregs from my purse; but he was warned that if he did not immediately "lose himself," he would be taken along to headquarters.

Again, evidently, I was on the way to a prison cell, and not now as a religious nonconformist only, but as a fugitive from "justice" of the old Russian brand. The jail was in sight, only a few rods away.

The officer intimated that three hundred rubles might keep me out of it. I told him I did not possess that much money. He then reduced his figures to two hundred fifty rubles, and again to two hundred. I had not that amount, nor was there any way I could get it, unless possibly some of my fellow church members of but a few days' acquaintanceship should be moved to supply it.

I requested that the police officer go with me, and I would undertake to borrow the sum named. He objected, saying that if I did not have the cash on my person, we would go on to headquarters; but before we reached that dread structure, he consented to do as I wished, and we took a cab to the home of one of my stranger friends.

When we came to the house, I left the cab, but the officer cautioned me not to go out of his sight. I rapped at the gate; and when the host came to open it, he was not slow to comprehend my situation.

How severe a mental struggle it may have cost this good man to decide to advance me a sum that must seem so large to a person of his means, was not evident from his manner; and after reëntering the house for a few moments, he again appeared, got into the carriage with us, and directed that we be driven to a bank.

While he was in the bank, my custodian and I waited in a restaurant near. As we ate, or pretended to eat, our *borshtch* — cabbage soup — the officer sought to convince me that he was not a bad fellow. It was customary, he affirmed, for police officers to get money in this manner. He even professed a disinterested regard for my welfare, and asked that I write him if ever I reached a place of safety. But I was content to bid him a final farewell when our deal was closed.

Not many months later, the amount this generous brother had lent to me was returned to him, and I had the satisfaction of receiving acknowledgment of the payment.

I was little concerned as to how the spoils were divided among the police officers, the old exile, and the ostensibly benign and honorable business man. I realized that not on such as these, nor on such measures as they employed, ought I to rely. I had subjected myself to danger, loss, anxiety, and compromise, in the attempt to get a passport, though a passport would have been useless without the special care of Him who had brought me over thousands of miles without a passport.

CHAPTER XVI

A FUTILE ATTEMPT AT FLIGHT

IN harmony with the advice of friends, I now engaged the Manchurian guide who had been recommended to me, to go with me by horseback to Mukden, about four hundred miles south, not far from the boundary line between Manchuria and China proper. This young man could speak the Russian language well enough to act as interpreter for me, as well as guide, I having no knowledge of Chinese.

Separated from Harbin by the railroad, is the little Manchurian village of Fudziadzian. There the Russian police had no jurisdiction; and I made my way thither, that I might be the safer while preparing to continue my flight. I afterwards learned that the Russian police did not always let lack of authority deter them from seizing one they wished to make a prisoner.

To reach this village, I must pass through a field where all sorts of offal had been thrown, including dead bodies of animals and even of human beings. There were open sewers, and almost every conceivable source of vile odors, which were more in evidence the nearer I came to the gate of the village.

My first business in the village was to visit the horse market. I found it crowded with dealers and customers, nearly all Manchurians. There was much bickering between the two classes, the owners praising their animals, and asking exorbitant prices for them, while prospective buyers berated them, and offered absurdly low prices.

When a dealer took the hand of a customer, and drew over it his long sleeve, that meant he was ready for business; and the price he then fixed was the lowest he was likely to accept. Any one who did not come to business after clasping hands with a dealer, put himself in great disfavor.

Adjacent to the market was a road where horses could be tested before a deal was closed. And there was need of testing them, for all the tricks of the professional horse trader were used to palm off worthless animals. Many of these animals had been drugged to make them appear spirited and in good flesh; some were balky, others vicious; few were strong enough for the jaunt I had in prospect.

Negotiations were so protracted by the circumlocution necessary in dealing with the owners, that I was obliged to spend three days in selecting two horses, together with saddles, riding whips, and feed, and getting

A NATIVE OF THE FAR NORTHERN PROVINCE OF YAKUTSK WITH HIS SADDLE PONY

the required papers made out. Any one found in Manchuria with a horse in his possession for which he cannot show a deed duly signed and witnessed, is liable to arrest as a thief.

My guide took me to the home of a family of his acquaintance, with whom I could stay at reasonable cost until we were ready to start on our journey. My repugnance for everything Asiatic, I here resolutely put aside, knowing that contact with Manchurians on the way would be unavoidable.

A young son of this family had worked for a number of years on a steamer running on the Sungari (Black) River from Harbin to northern Siberia, and had learned to speak Russian well enough to be understood. He did me valuable service by drawing a map of the route I was to take.

As the river was then frozen over, I could cross on the ice, instead of having to face the Russian guards at the bridges. My apparently fruitless sojourn at Harbin had prevented my beginning the journey before the ice formed.

In starting on my way, I had to go through old Harbin again; but coming from a Manchurian town, in company with a Manchurian, and being so bundled up as not to be readily distinguishable from one of that race, I was unnoticed by the police. Soon we were out on the open highway, and started off on a gallop.

The guide proved to be a poor horseman; and before we were well under way, his horse, being ill managed, fell into a ditch, laming himself, hurting the rider, and dislodging the baggage.

In half an hour, we were once more in our saddles. The roads were poor, but that did not impress me as a serious handicap.

A short distance outside the city were stationed the last of the Russian guard. I passed them without being accosted, doubtless because they mistook me for a Manchurian. I was beginning to feel jubilant at getting away from Harbin; but my guide was not at all jubilant. He lagged far behind; and when I waited for him to overtake me, he dismounted and led his horse. He complained that he was suffering from the effect of his fall, and that furthermore he was not dressed warmly enough for such weather. I induced him to remount, and we rode on for a little while.

Again and again this performance was repeated, the fellow becoming continually more spiritless. He talked of difficulties ahead — uncertainty of securing feed for our horses or food for ourselves, and what not; said he was sick; and finally could not be prodded any farther.

What could I do? To go on alone with the two horses was out of the question, and I could ill afford to abandon one. Then, too, to travel without guide or interpreter would be to attract much attention in making purchases and inquiring about the roads; and if I had a horse to care for, there would be less opportunity for concealment than if I had none.

I determined to return to the horse market, sell the animals, leave my baggage with friends, and start out afoot.

Though chagrined at the failure of my recent efforts, I was not disheartened.

I reached Fudziadzian again without difficulty; but the sale of the horses and equipment was not easily effected, and the amount I received when I did sell them was much less than I had paid.

After disposing of them, I ventured into Harbin, to spend one more night with the faithful friends there. Undeniably this was a rash thing to do; but the encouragement found in association with these good people, outweighed the danger incurred.

CHAPTER XVII

AFOOT AND ALONE

"TALL and small" were on their feet early the next morning, and soon I was ready for my pilgrimage. I dared not encumber myself with heavy clothing, though I knew that I should suffer from lack of such.

I carried a strong walking stick that a young son of the family had provided for me — a fortunate provision it proved to be — and in my small traveling bag was some European food to supplement the unpalatable Chinese food I should purchase on the way.

As I was about to start, my hostess proposed that I take with me a Chinese Testament that she had. I was very reluctant to add so much weight to my luggage, but the good woman insisted; and I acquiesced, solely in deference to her wishes. Erelong that volume served a purpose which neither she nor I had foreseen.

Mukden was my intended destination. That city was next after Harbin on the list given me by the good man who had marked out for me the seemingly reckless journey from the Caucasus to America. It was also on the only practicable route for me to follow — if indeed any route was practicable for a person in my circumstances.

The friends I was leaving could not express any hope that I should ever see Mukden; for the road led frequently across the railroad, which was under Russian control, though on Chinese territory, and was guarded by Russian soldiers.

I left a message to be sent to my parents in case no word came from me inside of three weeks, as a longer silence would indicate that

A Makeshift Tent on the Russian Steppes

I had been either captured or killed. Of the two fates, I dreaded the latter least. But I did not expect either. I set out assured that I should yet accomplish what I was undertaking.

On my horseback trip with the Manchurian guide, I had learned the safest road by which to leave the city, and I followed it "without let or hindrance." The wind was icy cold. My breath made a fringe of frost on my camel's-hair skating cap, which was drawn about my face, as a protection from both cold and observation.

As the last of the Russian factory buildings were disappearing from sight, I turned to bid farewell to what had been to me a city of perplexities. Then, as I hastened on, I saw coming toward me a company of men who I concluded were Russian soldiers. To elude them, I turned off onto the prairie; and they did not molest me. They may have supposed me to be a Manchurian; or, like many of the imperial Russian soldiers, ill fed and dissatisfied, themselves little better off than prisoners, they may not have been averse to letting one in similar plight better his condition if he could do so.

As I passed through the first village, the inhabitants displayed much curiosity. It is not improbable that they took for granted I was a fugitive; for only a few days before, several Russian soldiers had attempted to escape from Harbin, but had been captured not many miles away.

Snow was falling fast; and after leaving the village, I could not clearly distinguish the road. The nearness of the railroad was evidence that I was not far out of the way; but otherwise I should have preferred that the railroad had not been so near, because of the likelihood of encountering some of the guards.

Presently, turning my face to one side to avoid the cutting wind, I saw a Manchurian coming behind me. He was not particularly prepossessing, being bleary-eyed, like many of the Manchurians, as a result of the smoke from their open fires. But I was glad of the prospect of being with some one who knew the road, and he seemed equally pleased to have company. He could speak a few words of Russian; and these, augmented by signs, enabled us to carry on a fragmentary conversation.

Soon the man signified that he was going to take a footpath that branched off from the road. I asked what town lay in that direction; and he replied, Shwang-chang-puo. When I told him I was going to the same place, he took me by the arm, and drew me out of the road, making me understand that the trail over the prairie was preferable, being more direct. Certainly it was more desirable for me, in that it was farther from the railway.

On the highway, we often met caravans of Manchurian carts, with solid wooden wheels, each cart drawn by four to eight mules. They were hauling beans, millet, peanuts, and other foodstuffs to the railway for shipment.

In a Manchurian village, one meets more dogs than human beings. The dogs are a hungry looking lot; and with a few bits of bread, a stranger can often, though not always, make friends of a host of them.

In the towns that we passed through, I observed bright-colored paper ornaments in front of some of the buildings. My traveling companion informed me that these buildings were inns. I was soon to become more familiar with such places than was agreeable. About the middle of the afternoon, being chilled and hungry, we stopped at one of them, and called for a warm drink. The proprietor replied that he had none, nor did he have much food to offer, except roasted peanuts and a sort of bean paste; but these, with bread from my bag, made a fairly satisfactory lunch.

A score or so of villagers who sat about the place, inquired of my fellow traveler whether I was a runaway soldier. They examined me closely, even feeling of my clothing, but exhibited no ill will.

Cold as we had been out in the wind, we were colder in the inn; and after our lunch, we traveled on. My good comrade could not keep up with my accustomed pace, possibly in part because his Chinese shoes were not well adapted to walking. However, he knew the country well, and often led me on short cuts across the fields and through some of the numerous little cemeteries, thus saving me many miles of travel.

Twilight overtook us in a heavy snowstorm, which so hid the road that soon we lost it utterly. Still I urged the Manchurian along, even though we did not know where we were going; for there was no shelter in sight,

THE TROITZKO-SERGIEV MONASTERY

This is one of the holy places of Russia, to which pilgrimages are made, mostly afoot, by people from all parts of Russia.

and thinly clad as I was, I should have perished if I had not kept moving briskly.

Taking the course of least resistance, we let the storm drive us. In a short time, we came to a small clump of trees, among which were a few graves with rude stone monuments. Shielded from the storm by trees and monuments, we rested there for a little while, and tried to make out the directions. Then we staggered ahead.

After about half an hour, we came upon a road. We did not know whether it led in the way we should go; but we followed it, and before we had gone far, it brought us to a little village. We did not seek lodging there, for we felt impelled to push on. The one thing we wanted was, to learn the route. We met a young man on the deserted streets, and of him we made inquiry. He graciously went with us some distance, then gave us the instruction we needed.

We went some miles farther, when, through the darkness and the storm, the outlines of a building took form before us, only a few yards away. It was an unwelcome sight; for I recognized the structure as the barracks of a Russian railway guard. A soldier passed within reach of my hand. Happily, the night and the snow rendered me indistinguishable from an Asiatic.

Not long afterwards, we reached a small settlement, and we thought best to stay there for the night. Each house was inclosed by a mud wall eight or nine feet high. We sought to enter one of the yards, but the gate was locked. Another and another were the same. At last, we found one that was unlocked; but according to Manchurian usage, we must not approach within about two rods of the house unbidden. My guide called to the inmates, making known our desire to find lodgings. A voice from within replied that there was no room for us there.

We went outside the wall again. After a time, a cart came in sight, drawn by several mules. This we followed, and in its wake, gained entrance to an inn. The proprietor protested that his house was already full; but eventually we persuaded him to make room for us.

The inn, like most of the country houses, was built of bamboo, and plastered with mud. The window panes were of paper. For some minutes after entering, I could hardly breathe, because of the smoke from the big kettle that answered as a stove, and from the pipes of the occupants of the room. These pipes were made of bamboo, with clay bowls, and varied in length from less than a foot to more than two feet.

Place was assigned us on the platform that must do duty as table, chairs, and beds for the entire company. Soon the cook appeared, and prepared over the fire something akin to noodles, afterwards serving it in small bowls. Cook, food, and dishes all looked very unclean; but I had had no warm food since morning, and my vigorous boyish appetite still stayed by me. So, sitting cross-legged, like the Manchurians, I made my first attempt to manipulate a pair of chopsticks — thus affording considerable entertainment for the spectators.

Weariness and the warmth of the room made me feel disposed to sleep; but my success in that direction was not enhanced by the chatter of the other guests, nor by the thinness of the rush mat which was all that modified the hardness of the clay platform. Moreover, I was too chilled to sleep. My thoughtful guide, observing my restlessness, asked our host for a blanket for me; and a piece of an old bed comfort was brought. It gave inadequate protection from the cold drafts that came through the crevices in the walls; yet in time I fell asleep.

It must have been about three o'clock the next morning when I awoke because of the cold. We arose, paid the innkeeper the few cents charged for our supper and lodging, and took our leave. We hoped to reach Shwang-chang-puo before the next night.

The storm had abated, though there was still a strong wind. The moon looked down full-faced on the snow-covered region. Its light was sufficient to guide us, but the snow hid the road.

The wind went through my clothes as if they had been gauze. I soon became almost numb from cold. To combat it, we ran. From my eyes, smarting from the effects of the smoke at the inn, tears streamed down my cheeks, and froze there.

The conditions truly were not exhilarating; but I asked the pitying Father for courage and strength, and thanked Him for the kindly guide He had sent me, without whom I should have been much worse off.

As we hurried along over the creaking snow, I learned from my fellow pedestrian a few Manchurian words, and this little knowledge was afterwards very useful.

After some hours, our road crossed the Russian railway, near barracks; but presumably the guard saw in us only two natives, for we passed unchallenged — except for the dogs, which followed us a long way.

As they turned back, we saw ahead of us a wayside shrine, which denoted the probable proximity of a village. Within the shrine was a dish of rice intended for the spirits that were supposed to sojourn there, but appropriated by the birds. The religion of the Manchurians has to do principally with evading evil spirits, and appeasing those which cannot be evaded.

In the village not far beyond, we stopped at an inn to rest and warm ourselves. The inmates were too intent on their smoking, or too stupid, to heed our coming or going; and I was relieved at being unobserved.

I was more relieved when, later in the day, we came in sight of Shwang-chang-puo; for traveling was becoming very difficult, my muscles being stiff and sore.

A Manchurian Convict

The punishment of this man, condemned to spend the remainder of his life in a box, surpassed that of a Siberian exile.

To reach the city gate, we had to pass around a long wall. The shelter of this wall was most welcome.

Compared with other Manchurian towns I had seen, this one seemed ancient, but neat and orderly.

It lies near the Russian railway. Soon after entering it, I saw a European on the street; but as he apparently did not notice me, I felt little misgiving on his account. Later I espied a Russian soldier, and this was enough to admonish me that I should exercise caution about being seen.

We went into a small eating booth, where the warmth was most gratifying to our benumbed bodies. What my palate said to the unaccustomed foods, I could not hear, because of the louder cries of hunger.

Before I left Harbin, some of my friends there told me that in Shwang-chang-puo there was a native evangelist of our faith, who spoke a little Russian. I had taken his address, thinking he might help me to plan for the remainder of the journey. But in that strange Oriental city, how could I search out any one, without making myself dangerously conspicuous?

I decided to continue my journey; and my volunteer guide declared his intention to go along, although his only motive, so far as I could learn, was the purely unselfish one of looking after my welfare.

We started toward the south gate. Though we could converse but little, yet we smiled encouragement at each other; and I needed encouragement, for I was nearly exhausted.

As we were passing the last compound inside the wall, the guide excitedly caught hold of me, and pointing to the gateway, exclaimed, "Yesua, Yesua!" Then he pulled me into the yard, where there were several natives. Their bearing was genial, and the premises were exceptionally clean.

This was a Christian mission. My guide had discovered the fact by the sign over the gateway; and his exclamation "Yesua" was an attempt to speak the name "Jesus." The native evangelists here knew the one I had wished to find, and they directed us to his home. Half an hour's walk, with some inquiry by the way, brought us to the house.

A middle-aged man of amiable appearance, with his wife, welcomed us. Portraits that had been given to me in Harbin, of some of our missionaries in China, were an indication, to this good couple, that I had been associated with our people; and they appeared as happy to have me in their home, as I was to be in so hospitable a place.

My guide, seeing that I was now among friends, essayed to leave; but he was not permitted to go until he had received all due courtesies.

My host and hostess had been but a few years out of heathenism; yet the contrast between them and the non-Christians about them, was very marked. The little group of converts they had gathered, also gave proof of a marvelous transformation of character.

In our training school that this evangelist and his wife had attended, the students were not taught European customs in lieu of Oriental, except in so far as the latter were objectionable. Consequently the house in which I found myself a guest was not unlike those about it, except for its cleanliness.

The same was true of the food and clothing of the family. The staple articles of diet were millet, cabbage, and peanuts. To make the food palatable for myself, I was obliged to add salt, much to the amusement of the house-

A Peasant Family
The yoke alone would stamp this as a Russian outfit.

hold. The Manchurians, instead of salting their food in general, eat with it very salty cabbage.

My host and some of his friends seemed delighted with a chalk talk that I gave them, the former translating to those who did not understand any language I could speak. My singing also evidently pleased them. I could not pretend to an equal enjoyment of the dirge-like Manchurian music, all of which sounded alike to me, whether the occasion was a funeral or a wedding.

I applied myself to the study of Chinese, in order that I might better make my wants known when I should resume my journey.

The evangelist begged that I remain with him, learn the language, and do evangelistic work among the people. This proposition was not without appeal to me; but I knew that even my brief stay there was hazardous, for though I was in Chinese territory, any of the numerous Russian soldiers seen on the streets would not on that account hesitate to seize me, should they have a hint of my identity.

After a few days' recuperation, I started out once more on my perilous trip. My host proposed to accompany me a day's walk, to a village where some people lived who were studying the Bible with him.

In going through the city, I met, near the gate of the government building, my recent guide. He wore a uniform, having obtained a civil service commission. Though he could not well go with me now, he manifested the same brotherly interest in me as before.

The evangelist and I, after a walk of some twelve miles, reached the tiny village that we had set out for. Manchuria is much less densely populated than China proper, and its villages are fewer and smaller. The population of the one to which we were going was made up almost wholly of the various branches of one well-to-do family. They were converts of an evangelical church; and though they were not so well instructed as those I had just left, still their homes were a tribute to the work of Christian missions.

I shall perhaps not be criticized for asserting that the converts of our own missions give greater evidence of the transforming power of the gospel, than do those of any other missions I have visited — and I have visited those of many different churches.

We were received cordially by the villagers, and later were requested to conduct an evening service. Again I resorted to the use of crayon sketches to atone for my inability to speak the language. This manner of teaching quite captivated the little audience, and they too would fain have had me take up my permanent residence in Manchuria and teach the gospel.

In truth, what I saw, during this journey, of the influence of Christianity among heathen people, fully convinced me that foreign mission work is worthy the best efforts of any young man. The world offers nothing to surpass it.

The patriarch of the little clan made us his guests for the night, and all the men of the settlement came and slept with us. That was in accordance with their ideas of social ethics.

The morning was creeping over the wall of the compound when I bade them adieu, and once more started out, staff in hand. The evangelist walked a little distance with me, then I went on — alone. The full meaning of that word "alone" is not easily learned.

In less than two hours, I had lost the road; but I found it again after a time. Then I

CAUCASIAN TRIBESMEN
There are more than twenty different races of people in the Caucasus, and they vary widely.

(241)

discovered that I was too close to the railway, and must quickly take a different route.

This program was often repeated. The map made for me by the young man at whose home I stayed while preparing for the journey, was of much benefit to me, but it did not contain sufficient details; and when I endeavored to obtain information of Manchurians along the way, not only was I hampered by ignorance of their language, but some apparently found malicious pleasure in giving misinformation.

But though I often missed my way, I seemed never to miss any of the dogs. They assailed me in droves. In such cases, I plied my walking stick with good effect.

CHAPTER XVIII

ENCOUNTERING RUSSIAN GUARDS

REACHING a village late in the evening, cold and tired, I was besieged, in the inn, by a curious crowd, who felt my clothes, my pockets, and my traveling bag. Some spoke a few words of Russian, and they began to question me. They gave me no opportunity to sleep.

Then I thought of the Chinese New Testament that I had unwillingly put into my bag at Harbin. I learned that some of the men could read, and I asked one to read aloud to the company. Soon he had attentive listeners. I have seldom witnessed more reverential attention to the Scriptures, in any land.

Notice being thus diverted from me, I lay down on the brick bed, made a pillow of my shoes, and with no covers, tried to sleep.

Repeatedly thereafter, in other villages, I employed this device to get a little rest. And I needed the rest, for I walked many miles each day.

In shunning roads near the railway, more than once I paid for my caution by being obliged to "back track." Often I climbed hills to get a view of the roads. Sometimes I could find no cue to the route, and could only pray Heaven to lead, and blindly wander on. And verily Heaven heard.

The increasing cold, though it added to my discomfort, was an advantage to me, in that it caused ice to form thicker on the rivers; and now I could cross on the ice without fear of its breaking, and thus could keep clear of the bridges, with their Russian guards.

Sometimes, in crossing thus, I had difficulty in scaling the bluffs on the farther side. Nor did I escape the Russian soldiers altogether. In a little village that I came to at one time as I left the river, one of these dreaded representatives of the despotism from which I was fleeing, caught sight of me.

I went into an eating house, knowing that Russian soldiers in uniform were prohibited from entering Manchurian buildings. He stopped at the doorway, and ordered food brought to him. Would he wait there to catch me as I left the place?

I ate with relish the dumplings served for me, notwithstanding the prospect awaiting me outside, and the smoke and dirt within.

My meal finished, I ventured on the street again, but saw no more of the soldier.

My feet had become so sore from walking, that I could hardly spur myself on. Moreover, not far outside the village, I found myself almost completely shut in by swamps and high bluffs. The only way I could proceed was by a long bridge, at the farther end of which was a Russian military post. Retreat would give no assurance of safety, and would be most disheartening. I decided to go ahead.

With feigned nonchalance, I started toward the bridge, taking the precaution to draw my knit cap close about my face. The natives gazed at me in obvious astonishment, rightly surmising, no doubt, that I was a fugitive, and marveling that I should walk into the very arms of my captors.

I met only one soldier, and he merely glanced carelessly at me as I passed. Thus I went on unhindered.

This escape from what had seemed like inevitable capture, gave me new hopefulness; and despite the crippled condition of my feet, I hastened forward.

According to my map, the next city was not so far but I might possibly reach it that night;

and the cities furnished more secure hiding places than did the small villages. But as darkness began to steal over the snowy fields, and the city was not yet in sight, I knew that I could not see to keep the road much longer. Then I determined to follow the railroad; for as I had so lately passed a military post, there would not be another for some miles.

Natives warned me not to stay out after dark, for fear of bandits. Still I went on.

Out of the darkness came sounds as from a human abode. There were lights also. I went toward them, but my advance was soon blocked by a wall. I hunted for a gateway, and found one, but it was closed and locked. Likewise another and still another. Finally I came to one that opened to an inn, and there I entered.

Before I had begun to eat the typical Manchurian supper that was put before me, the news had spread that a European was in the inn. Men and boys flocked into the dingy room, and pressed about me. But by that time, I had become accustomed to such a performance; and in spite of it, I slept.

When I awoke, the air of the room was suffocating. My head ached, and my eyes were inflamed by the smoke. Cattle had been brought into the room, that they might be protected from the cold, and to add to the warmth of the inmates.

To get away from these surroundings, I started out into the night, though my feet were so sore and my joints so stiff that I could not make my usual headway. Nor could I see the road; but by means of my staff, I felt my way along the railroad.

The figure of a human being emerged from the darkness. I was certain that he was a guard; but the darkness, though it did not conceal me, did conceal my race, and I was permitted to pass.

Then a horseman was heard near. It is not improbable that he was a member of a band of Mongolian marauders. But again I was unmolested.

At dawn, a fog enveloped the country. Seeing only a few feet ahead of me, I came unexpectedly upon a barrack. Several dogs rushed out, snarling ominously. Fearing not so much the dogs as the soldiers, I beat ahead as fast as I could; but the brutes kept after me. I still think with regret of the walking stick I broke in pieces on them.

Before the soldiers located the din of the dogs, I had contrived to get away, and was hidden by the fog. Thus the same fog that had betrayed me into danger, delivered me from it.

In about an hour, I was at the gate of the city. People were coming out to their work in the fields. With them were mules, donkeys, water buffaloes, cows, goats, sheep, and dogs. It was a satisfaction, after my solitary night walk, to see human beings again.

A Mongolian Plainsman
He may almost be said to spend his life on the back of his horse.

Our evangelist at Shwang-chang-puo had given me the address of a Christian shopkeeper in this city, and I readily located him. When I mentioned the evangelist to him, his face expressed genuine pleasure, and he received me with a cordiality that was both Oriental and Christian.

I was taken to a guest room that was in strong contrast to the inns at which I had stopped. Instead of straw mats, there were beautiful carpets. The raised platform was provided with bedding, which was rolled back against the wall in the daytime. The premises entire were marked by the neatness that invariably distinguishes the homes of Christians from those of the heathen.

After a few hours' rest, I started out again, edging my way through streets teeming with buffalo and mule carts, and with men smoking long pipes.

The next day, the road again led across the railway. I saw no way of avoiding it; for in all other directions, high hills closed me in.

Two Russian soldiers accosted me, demanding my passport. As I had none, they talked together as to what was to be done with me. It was suggested that perhaps I was a runaway soldier. They themselves were experiencing the hardships of a soldier's life under the rule of the czar, and they may have had a fellow feeling for one whom they supposed to be fleeing from such a life. Whatever their reason, they signaled me to pass on.

To what influence, natural or supernatural, I owe my deliverance from dangers throughout that journey of several thousand miles, I am willing the reader shall judge.

More and more my aching feet protested against going farther. I wrapped them in cloths, and tried to keep up my daily mileage; but I could not now make more than fifteen or twenty miles a day.

Once a Manchurian invited me to ride in his cart, and I did so; but it jolted so violently, because of the irregularities in the huge wooden wheels, that I was not sorry when our routes diverged, and I must again walk.

Many hundred miles still lay between me and Shanghai, the last milepost on the trans-Asiatic journey mapped out for me. Yet, most of the time, I felt confident that I should ultimately reach it.

One morning, after traveling several miles before sunrise, I came to a town where there was a Christian mission, as I had been told by the Christian merchant whose guest I had been some days before; but there was little ground for thinking that I could find it.

I went into an inn — a comparatively clean one; and as many of the guests of the night before had already gone, I hoped to have better opportunity to rest than ordinarily. But the heat of the room, after the severe cold outside, caused a painful prickling of my flesh. Then, too, I was alternately feverish and chilly.

A Manchurian who was in the room, seemed very benevolently disposed, and did what he could for my comfort. I endeavored to tell him of my quest for the mission; but my very limited vocabulary apparently did not suffice to make me understood.

The man left the inn. Soon afterwards he came back; and beckoning me to go with him, he took me to a mission building where two young natives were in charge, who I learned were Catholics. They were very amiable. I ate with them the most appetizing meal I had eaten in Manchuria.

The head teacher spoke some English; and in the course of our conversation, he told me that his assistant, though his services were of much value, appeared to be unable to give up the use of intoxicants. The converts of the Catholic missions, in some instances, use intoxicants more than do the heathen. Yet I could but acknowledge the good effect of their teaching in the line of neatness.

This head teacher's knowledge of English enabled him to give me more information in reference to my route than any one else I had met. He told me that the next town on the railway was a Russian military fortification. Hence I knew that there was need of being most discreet.

As I was leaving the mission, a heavy cart drawn by five horses came along. Accepting this as a guide, I followed it till I reached a place where the road had been flooded, and a wide field of ice spread before us. The cart then turned to the north. As my route lay in general to the south, I kept on across the ice. Footprints showed that others had gone that way before me.

Having crossed the ice and climbed the bank beyond, I found a great stretch of sand. There was no trail, walking was difficult, no sign of a shelter could be seen, and night was not far away. The hills beyond were covered with a network of brush and roots of fallen trees, which signified that all this space was under water when the river was high.

I struck off to the northwest, to get away from the sand waste; and after some time, I

One of the Scenes of Greatest Danger

came to a road that I thought might be the one I should take. Then on ahead I caught sight of the cart that I had followed from the city. Again I trudged along in its wake.

We were now going toward the west, whereas I should go south; but to the south was a high bridge, and I dared not go near it, because of its Russian guard.

Continuing to the west, I crossed the river on the ice, and took the road that wound up the steep bank on the other side. Presently I came upon a little village in a nook of the hills. Shielded as it was from the cold wind, it was a real bit of summerland. Men were threshing grain by driving horses over it. The scene was an attractive one, except for the hogs and the dirt—both prominent features of Manchurian life.

This was the end of the road. What should I do now? I had gained but little ground all the afternoon, and I did not want to go back over the route I had been traveling. I started across the fields, hoping to reach a road that would lead in the direction I ought to go.

Without warning, I found myself at the edge of an old Russian fort. Hot and cold chased each other up and down my spine. The fort evidently had been abandoned; but not far away I could see a garrison of soldiers, and they could see me if they should glance that way, though probably they could not see that I was a European.

I scrambled down a steep bank on the farther side, and came out on a road. There I overtook an old man, and of him I inquired

A Village Priest
He ekes out his small income by tilling his small piece of ground.

the way to the next city. He pointed forward; and I pushed on, to find a place to stay that night. Ahead of us I could see some men driving mules loaded with brush, and soon I caught up with them. My lacerated feet and tired muscles rebelled against being driven any farther; but I rallied all my reserve energy, and hastened along the darkening road.

After a time, I came up with a caravan of Manchurians taking produce to market. I thought best to join them, in order to get entrance to the city when we should reach it; and they raised no objection. I chafed at the slowness of their gait, yet I did not think that I should do well to go on alone.

We met a company of Manchurian soldiers; but I was not in the danger from them that I was from Russian soldiers.

Over hills and through valleys we went, and finally, rounding a hill late at night, came into a town. I helped the men of the caravan to put up their horses, then went with them to a long, barn-like building where they were to spend the night.

There was a Manchurian military training camp in this town, and many of the soldiers were in the inn gambling. They were quite friendly; but their very friendliness was wearisome, for I greatly needed rest. I took from my bag my Chinese New Testament, and asked one of the company to read aloud. This he did, while the others listened intently —and I slept.

Before another dawn, I was again on the road. About noon, I must cross the Russian railway, not far from a military post; and I could see that a little way ahead, the road, winding about, again crossed the track, this time close to the barracks. I stopped at a country inn to consider what to do. Even there I was not safe, as soldiers from the post were likely to be about.

There was no way for me to go except ahead, and ahead I went. As I approached the crossing, I saw that an officer and a civilian were on guard. The former halted me, and asked where I was going.

Instantly the thought came to me that I should appear unafraid, but make no reply. The officer then told the civilian to repeat the question in German, and he did so. Still I was silent, though I understood him perfectly.

Next the interpreter spoke in English — very poor English, however. I replied, in English, that I was an evangelist, and had been visiting a mission station, and was now on my way to the next town. This was all true, though it was not the whole truth.

I suspect that the interpreter did not understand English well enough to know what I had said, but disliked to confess his ignorance to his superior. He recited to him, in Russian, an absurd story about my having been sent on a tour of inspection of some sort.

A SMALL PORTION
OF THE NIZHNI NOVGOROD FAIR

The diversity of goods offered for sale at this great fair, formerly held annually, gave it widespread fame.

The audacity of the fiction and the perplexity of the officer so diverted my mind that I almost forgot, for the moment, the peril of my situation; and doubtless my unconcerned manner had to do with convincing the guard that I had all due authority back of me. I must have looked more like a hobo than like any sort of inspector.

The guard seemed not to think of asking for proof of my commission, or even for my passport. After a few moments' hesitancy, he gave me leave to go on — and I did not need to be urged.

To some, this might seem like a mere novel adventure; but it was much more than that to me. My freedom and even my life were at stake; and when the incident was over, and I realized what a position I had been in, I was so overwhelmed I could scarcely stand.

As I passed through the next village, an innkeeper hailed me, remarking that the sun was already setting. But I went on. Dogs attacked me in such numbers and so viciously that I almost used up my second walking stick on them.

Walking was torture to my bleeding feet, and I knew that I could not keep up much longer. Still I was resolved not to stop until I had passed Kwanchengtze, the terminus of the Russian railway, which I was sure must be a place of special danger, because of the strong guard stationed there. A few miles beyond that was Changchun, where the Japanese railway begins.

The beauty of the night was an inspiration. I lost all trace of the road, but kept the general direction by the aid of the stars.

Down deep ravines, across marshes, and through bamboo thickets, I struggled on. I heard dogs barking, and shots fired. Whence these sounds came, or whether they had to do with me, I did not know. One thought dominated my mind — Changchun. I did not have strength to think of anything else.

About midnight or later I came to higher ground. The air was colder, the stars were hidden, and a sleet beat in my face. I did not know which way to go. Across the desert of snow, I saw carts coming toward me. I waited till they came along, and then, inquiring of the drivers, learned that they were going the same way I wished to go. For hours I followed them along the winding road. After the lights of the Russian railway terminal came in sight, the cartmen turned off on another road; but I continued toward the station.

I almost held my breath as I passed the buildings, each moment expecting that a watchman would step out from the shadows. But I saw none; and at daybreak, I reached the first station of the Japanese railway — Changchun.

Knowing that the Japanese were allied with the Russians, I kept away from their part of the town, though it looked much more

A CHINESE CITY STREET

inviting than the Manchurian section. I entered an inn, in hope of finding a place to rest; but it offered no such boon.

I had walked continuously for thirty hours, and felt that I could go no farther. The pain from the torn flesh of my feet was sickening. In my extremity, I even contemplated attempting to board a train for Mukden, although that would have implied almost certain arrest. I went to the station, but found that no train was to leave until late in the evening.

Praying for guidance, again I sought a place where I might rest. Suddenly my attention was attracted by the sign, "British and Foreign Bible Society." Those words meant to me renewed hope.

CHAPTER XIX

A HAPPY TRANSITION

THE elderly Chinese in charge of the establishment could not understand what I said to him; but he tried to make me comfortable.

Later a young man came in, who spoke a little English; and when, with him to act as interpreter, the older man learned that I wished to find a quiet place to spend the night, he mentioned an English mission in the outskirts of the town, and volunteered to take me there. Early in the evening, we set out. It was about as much as I could do to keep up with the nimble Oriental.

On reaching the mission, we learned that the superintendent was absent; but an English gentlewoman welcomed me very graciously, and as supper was in readiness, I was taken directly to the dining room. There I was introduced to a guest, Mr. Morgan Palmer, a man perhaps thirty-five or forty years old.

As I thought best to give a brief account of myself before accepting further hospitality, I told, in few words, of my exile, my endeavor to reach America, and my need of rest. Our hostess assured me that I was free to remain where I was as long as I might desire to do so.

Mr. Palmer was restless; and soon he rose abruptly, came to me, seized me by the arm, and announced that I must go with him. His residence, he said, would be a more suitable place for me, being less public.

Two horses — one of which he had ridden, and a servant the other — stood at the door; for he had been on the point of leaving some minutes before I arrived, but had yielded to an invitation to stay for supper. He afterwards expressed his conviction that the delay was decreed by Providence.

Despite the remonstrances of our hostess, he hurried me out of doors, designated which horse I should mount, and we rode off. I did not feel quite positive as to whether I was to be taken to a retired place to rest, as represented, or landed again in a dungeon.

After a ride of some miles, we stopped in front of a large gate. Guards stood at attention on each side. Mr. Palmer remarked that they were not "black angels" — a term I had used in speaking of the Russian prison guards — but his private attendants. In the compound, servants took our horses, and waited upon us.

The house was an old Manchurian structure, not elegant, but interesting. My host ordered a bath prepared for me, and some of his own clothes substituted for my worn and soiled ones.

After supper, I observed that servants were improvising a small bed — for me, I supposed; but instead, it was for Mr. Palmer, and I was to occupy his bed. Protests availed nothing.

My emotions were perhaps akin to those of Sojourner Truth, who, on the first night after her liberation from slavery, not once supposing that the "beautiful, high, white bed" in the room where she was put was intended for her, crawled under the bed to sleep.

Mr. Palmer had been several years in China. In the earlier of those years, he taught in the Peking University; but he was now inspector for the government salt administration in the provinces of Kirin and Heilung-chiang. The salt industry is a government monopoly, importation of that commodity being prohibited.

In the book "A Thousand Miles of Miracle in China," is told the part acted by this energetic American in the rescue of missionaries in the interior of China at the time of the Boxer uprising. But these things I did not learn till later.

The first night in that blissful haven, I could sleep but little, so affected was I by the change in my situation. I remained there for a fortnight. My host went about his business each day, leaving me to rest, read, or do whatever I would; but the evenings we spent together, and most congenially.

Still I knew that I was liable to capture there, for Russians might at any time call at the house, or my presence might in other ways become known to the Russian consul.

One evening, Mr. Palmer, knowing that I wished to reach Shanghai, suggested a plan by which possibly I might accomplish the journey. A hundred miles or so away, in the city of Kirin, lived a German who was known to have helped refugees to get from place to place. Mr. Palmer proposed to send an attendant with me to interview this man. As we could reach the place by the Chinese railway, a passport would not be required.

A HAPPY TRANSITION 267

The next morning, my host accompanied me to the Chinese railway station, and purchased tickets for me and the servant who was to go with me. The train was full, and a howling crowd outside were trying to get on board. We succeeded in getting standing room, but many were not so fortunate.

Reaching Kirin, we took a carette to the home of the man we sought. He was quite affable. Because of my speaking the German language, he apparently took for granted that I was a German; and he explained that he was connected with an organization whose object it was to help fellow countrymen reach the fatherland. He had funds at his disposal for that purpose, and operated a sort of "underground railway" across the hills, with buffalo carts as vehicles. He did not claim that this method of travel was safe. Indeed, he admitted that serious mishaps sometimes occurred to persons traveling thus.

But a hitch in negotiations developed. When the man learned that I did not expect to go to Germany and join the German army, he lost all interest in me.

I could only go back to Mr. Palmer's home and seek to evolve another plan of operation.

Mr. Palmer was disposed to write to our missionaries in Mukden, in reference to my future, and this he did. After that, he was obliged to be away from home for a number of days; and at his suggestion, I took a horseback ride each evening during his absence, attended by one of his servants, the darkness shielding me from observation. Russian-like, I might almost be said to have grown up on a horse, and I gloried in that form of recreation. Thus I was recuperating strength while awaiting developments.

Soon after my host's return, one of our Mukden missionaries also arrived at the place,

JUMPING THE ROPE
In Russia, only skilled horsemen are accounted as men.

The Old City of Mukden

in response to the letter sent him. He was on his way to Harbin, but designed to come back; and it was arranged that he should bring my baggage along. Then I was to go with him to Mukden.

It was a real trial for me to bid good-by to Mr. Palmer, and his regret at our parting evidently was no less than mine.

In company with my latest-found friend, I made the journey to Mukden by the Japanese railway. At each large station, Japanese officers eyed us quizzically, but each surprised us by making no demand for passports.

I spent the Sabbath quietly at the mission. Across the street was the Japanese consulate, and my host was solicitous lest I should be seen by some of the *attachés.*

The officers of the mission provided me with funds, trusting to a satisfactory adjustment later — which was duly effected; and thus equipped, I took train on the Chinese railway for Shanghai, four days distant.

CHAPTER XX

A PRISONER OF WAR

A NEW sense of freedom came to me, as I was no longer in momentary expectation of a call for my passport. The journey was not unpleasant, the trains being fairly clean. About one third of the passengers were Europeans and Americans.

As we went farther south, the contrast with Manchuria was marked. The population is much more dense, and the Chinese people are puny in comparison with the Manchurians.

On reaching Shanghai, I engaged one of the rickshas that beset me, the coolie who drew it pretending to know the address I gave him; but he wandered about for hours before he found our mission headquarters.

News of my coming had preceded me from Mukden. Afterwards I learned that an experience with an impostor some time before, had made our missionaries here skeptical about the truthfulness of my representations; but their bearing toward me gave no intimation of their suspicions.

As I was sinking to sleep that night in a room at the mission, there came to my ears the words of the following hymn, sung by one of the residents of the mission compound:

> "Be not dismayed, whate'er betide;
>   God will take care of you.
> Beneath His wings of love abide;
>   God will take care of you.
>
> "Through days of toil, when heart doth fail,
>   God will take care of you.
> When dangers fierce your path assail,
>   God will take care of you.
>
> "No matter what may be the test,
>   God will take care of you.
> Lean, weary one, upon His breast;
>   God will take care of you."

There was but one more name on the list of cities by which my route had been outlined ere I fled from my home in the Caucasus. That name was San Francisco.

Most of the steamers plying between San Francisco and Shanghai carried the flag of one of the allies of imperial Russia; and on board such craft, I should be almost certain to be rearrested. That would imply return to exile — or death, which would be a less grievous calamity.

In six weeks, however, a United States steamer, the China, was scheduled to sail; and

I was assured that whatever might be the alliances of the United States, she would not deliver up to a despotic power any person whose only offense was that he worshiped God "after the way which they call a sect." Acts 24:14, A. R. V.

I waited the six weeks for the American steamer. In the meantime, the activities of the missionaries, and the marvelous results seen, deeply interested me. Some of our missionaries urged that I remain in China and join them in their work. Others comprehended that I would not have there the government protection that I would have in America.

Aside from the matter of personal safety, there was another consideration that deterred me from accepting the proposition to remain in the Orient. That was the conviction that I ought to complete the course indicated by our venerable minister in the Caucasus, which I had been enabled to follow thus far notwithstanding seemingly impassable obstacles.

Yet mission effort in China appealed very strongly to me. Surely there is nothing to which the energy and ability of a young person can better be directed. Just one thought restrains me from returning to that country now, to devote my life to proclaiming the gospel that has wrought so remarkable a change in the lives of a few individuals among China's millions. That one restraining thought is — nearly two hundred million souls in my own native Russia who are in the darkness of Greek Catholicism, to whom I hope soon to go with the message of salvation.

As the time drew near for me to leave China, warning came from the American consul, that I must take special precautions to avoid observation when I should start for the steamer, as the Russian consular agents would be watching for deserters — with whom I might be classed.

Accordingly, it was agreed that, instead of going to the steamer station, whence a launch took passengers to the vessel, several miles out in the bay, I should go by railway to a suburb, Woosung, and from that point by motor boat to the vessel.

Some of our missionaries went with me to the station where I was to take a train for Woosung; and while waiting there, we all noticed that a man was watching us. To determine whether he was spying upon me, we

A Section of China's Great Wall

left the station; and soon after, we saw him on the street. We did not return to the station until we had barely time to board the train; and thus we eluded the pseudo sleuth. It was well for me that he was not an adept at his business.

From Woosung, we hastened to the protection of the Stars and Stripes floating over the steamer. Most of our missionaries at headquarters came off to spend the evening with me on board, as a warm friendship had developed between us; and the occasion was the happiest I had known for what seemed to me like a long time.

When I awoke next morning, Shanghai was no longer in sight, and the China was making good headway toward the land of liberty.

At about eleven o'clock, a vessel was sighted in the distance, approaching us; and when it came near, a shot was fired from one of its guns. As we did not stop, a shell followed. Our captain, though he knew that no craft had a right to intercept a United States vessel thus, could only exercise the discretion that is declared to be the greater part of valor; for our pursuer was a man-of-war, flying the Australian colors. A launch came alongside, bringing soldiers from the man-of-war; and these were stationed at various places aboard the China.

The lieutenant in command of the launch demanded our vessel's passenger list. The captain demurred, but was compelled to yield. All the men booked as Germans or Austrians were put aboard the launch. Of all others, proof of nationality was required.

I stated that I was a Russian; but as I could produce no passport, I was lowered into the launch, a prisoner of war, and taken aboard the man-of-war.

I knew that the next move on the part of my captors, so far as I was concerned, would be to hand me over to Russia's representatives at some port near; and that involved all I had sought to escape by my flight.

Resolved to make all possible effort to save myself from such a fate, I asked for an interview with the commander of the warship. This was granted; and I repeated my claim to exemption from seizure, on the ground that I was a Russian. The officer replied that he would find out whether I was a Russian; and he sent for one of his engineers, who was of that nationality.

My pronunciation, together with my familiarity with Russian geography and customs, quickly convinced the man that I had spoken truthfully, and he so reported to the commander. Thereupon the latter, jocosely referring to my lack of a passport, ordered that I be taken back to the China, where the lieutenant still remained, and that my baggage be searched, by way of further establishing my status.

I remembered that there was at least one article in my baggage which would help to confirm my contention — the volume of Russian poems I had purchased at a bookstand when crossing Siberia as a wounded soldier.

Again on board the American steamer, I was delivered over to my captor, who commissioned some of his men to watch me till my baggage should be examined. As a vent for my agitation, I went to the piano in the social hall, where a matronly woman was sitting whom I had previously met; and with her playing an accompaniment, I sang.

Glancing toward the doorway, my eyes met those of the colonial lieutenant; but he turned away, descended to his launch, and returned to his ship. Again I was semi-free.

The Golden Gate, "The Gateway to Freedom"

This irregular procedure on the part of the commander of the Australian man-of-war, called forth fitting protest from the United States military authorities, and the colonial government made suitable amends. American newspapers at the time — March and April, 1916 — commented spiritedly on the occurrence.

A quiet passage to Honolulu, where I spent the day of waiting with missionaries to whom I had letters of introduction, then five more days at sea, and we passed through the Golden Gate — the gateway to freedom!

CHAPTER XXI

LIKE A DREAM

SOME of our people in Shanghai had preannounced to friends in California my arrival in San Francisco. Consequently, when I left the dock in that city, I was not alone in a strange land; for as I came off the steamer, I was met by E. W. Farnsworth, whose name and genial face are known to many thousands of our people throughout the United States.

He took me to his home in Oakland; but the shock occasioned by my seizure on shipboard, in addition to the deprivations and exposure of preceding months, had left me in such condition of health that after a few days, it was thought best for me to go to the St. Helena Sanitarium, up in the beautiful Napa County hills.

But even there I was not in Paradise. Fellow patients and others apparently thought to manifest their sympathy for me by asking me to rehearse the experiences I had recently passed through. I endeavored to put those things out of my mind, for the mention or thought of them was torture to me. At night,

I would awake in terror from a dream of being captured by "black angels"; and hardly could I realize that I had merely been dreaming. Then when I became composed enough to go to sleep again, it was only to live over once more all the horrors I had endured or feared since the night when I was thrust into a vile cell at the Odessa police station.

A happy incident in connection with my short sojourn at the sanitarium was a visit to the former home of Mrs. E. G. White. As a child in Russia, I had heard of her extraordinary career, and had wished that I might see her. Now it was my privilege to become acquainted with her son and his family; and the friendship of these Christian people was indeed a comfort to me after the loneliness of the preceding year and a quarter.

The parents of one of our missionaries in China sent a request that I visit them at their home in the little town of Mountain View, California. This I did; but there also kindly people gave me no opportunity to get my thoughts off the distressing ordeals which to some were little more than a diverting story.

An earnest-faced man whom I met at Mountain View — Mr. George O. Wellman, a member of our church there — with his dear little wife, seemed to comprehend my situation; and they authoritatively informed me that I was to take up my abode in their quiet home in the outskirts of the town, and there remain until I had regained normal strength.

To accept such protracted hospitality from strangers, I thought, would be an imposition on their generosity; but my excuses were waved lightly aside, and I was playfully told to obey orders.

I did not think of this invitation as implying more than a sojourn of a few weeks with these unselfish people; but eventually I realized that they had opened not only their home but also their hearts to me, and they have been to me truly father and mother ever since. Thus the Saviour's promise to any who should leave loved ones for His sake, was fulfilled to me.

Erelong, too, I received letters from my beloved parents in Russia, in response to those sent to them.

Yet I was "a man without a country." I was an exile still.

Then came news which startled the whole world — imperial Russia had given place to

Nicholas Romanov, the Last of the Czars, in Exile

a republic. And at the head of that republic was the man to whom largely I owed my removal from Siberia — Kerensky, the young socialist leader.

Full religious liberty was assured throughout Russia. All religious exiles were now

THE ANCIENT CITY OF TOBOLSK, THE BIBLICAL TUBAL.
To this place the Russian ex-monarch was
finally banished.

freed. This included Gorelic, and all our other faithful members who were in banishment for the Word's sake.

I was no longer a refugee. Instead, the czar under whose rule I had been banished, was himself an exile. His place of banishment was not far from where mine had been.

But soon followed the counter revolution, and the many months during which I could get no word from my dear people in the Caucasus, and knew not but they had fallen victims to those times of upheaval.

Again news came—good news. All my family were still living. And they sent greetings to all my new friends in America. I hope that includes you.

Not long after my arrival in California, there came to me, through my foster father, a privilege which I had greatly desired for years—that of supplementing my European school course with study in one of our American schools; and as I write these words, I have just received my degree from Pacific Union College.

Many times, during my imprisonment and exile, and while I was a fugitive, I found assurance in that verse from the fiftieth psalm, "Call upon Me in the day of trouble: I will deliver thee, and thou shalt glorify Me." God has fully verified for me that promise of deliverance; and by His grace, I will not fail of my part,—to glorify Him.

The dark story that I have related to you is to me now much like a dream. Yet one

On Pacific Union College Farm

feature of it stands out clear and strong in my mind — clearest and strongest at those points where the conditions were most discouraging; and that one feature is, the blessedness and reality of companionship with Jesus. I do not now dread any hardships that a wise, tender Saviour may permit to come upon me in the future; but infinitely worse than shackles and prison bars would be the loss of that precious fellowship.

Now, as I prepare to return to the land of my birth — one of the most needy yet most fruitful portions of the wide gospel field — instead of saying "Good-by" to you, I will invite you to "come over and help us" — help us to make known to many perplexed souls in that great country the loving Father who has given evidence, in the experiences recorded in this little volume, of His constant, personal care for each one of His children.

TEACH Services, Inc.
PUBLISHING

We invite you to view the complete
selection of titles we publish at:
www.TEACHServices.com

We encourage you to write us
with your thoughts about this,
or any other book we publish at:
info@TEACHServices.com

TEACH Services' titles may be purchased in
bulk quantities for educational, fund-raising,
business, or promotional use.
bulksales@TEACHServices.com

Finally, if you are interested in seeing
your own book in print, please contact us at:
publishing@TEACHServices.com

We are happy to review your manuscript at no charge.

www.ingramcontent.com/pod-product-compliance
Lightning Source LLC
Chambersburg PA
CBHW070539160426
43199CB00014B/2302